U0565236

本书编写组 编

中华优秀传统文化书系

Excellent Chinese Traditional Culture
The Works of Mencius

孟子

（二）

山东画报出版社

出版说明

　　山东是儒家文化的发源地，也是中华优秀传统文化的重要发祥地，在灿烂辉煌的中华传统文化"谱系"中占有重要地位。用好齐鲁文化资源丰富的优势，扎实推进中华优秀传统文化研究阐发、保护传承和传播交流，推动中华优秀传统文化创造性转化、创新性发展，是习近平总书记对山东提出的重大历史课题、时代考卷，也是山东坚定文化自信、守护中华民族文化根脉的使命担当。

　　为挖掘阐发、传播普及以儒家思想为代表的中华优秀传统文化，推动中华文明与世界不同文明交流互鉴，山东省委宣传部组织策划了"中华优秀传统文化书系",并列入山东省优秀传统文化传承发展工程重点项目。书系以儒家经典"四书"(《大学》《中庸》《论语》《孟子》)为主要内容,对儒家文化蕴含的哲学思想、人文精神、教化思想、道德理念等进行了现代性阐释。书系采用权威底本、精心校点、审慎译注,同时添加了权威英文翻译和精美插图,是兼具历史性与时代性、民族性与国际性、学术性与普及性、艺术性与实用性于一体的精品佳作。

前言

　　《孟子》是记录孟子及其弟子言行以及孟子游说各国国君、同各派思想家进行辩论的语录体著作。它集中反映了孟子的思想体系，同时保留了不少战国时期的历史信息，为我们理解孟子、走进百家争鸣那个时代提供了基本材料。

一、孟子其人其书

　　孟子，名轲，战国时期邹（今山东邹城）人。相传孟子是鲁国贵族孟孙氏后裔，幼年丧父，家庭贫穷，迁居至邹，由其母抚养长大。

孟子是继孔子、曾子、子思之后儒家学派又一位重要人物，被后世誉为"亚圣"，与孔子并称"孔孟"。其生卒年不见详载，杨伯峻考证为约公元前385年到公元前304年。孟子在书中说："予未得为孔子徒也，予私淑诸人也。"孟子以继承孔子衣钵为己任，但未能言明其师是何人。关于孟子之师，学界有所争论，但多以《史记·孟子荀卿列传》所载为是，即"受业子思之门人"，也就是说孟子是孔子的孙子——子思的再传弟子，可谓是儒门正宗。所以其书以继承发扬孔子的思想为要，正所谓"退而与万章之徒序《诗》《书》，述仲尼之意，作《孟子》七篇"。

《孟子》的主要内容来源于孟子自是无疑，可其具体作者，学界有不同认识，比如孟子自著；孟子门下弟子万章和公孙丑之徒在孟子死后所著等，其中以在孟子生前由弟子辅助所著最能为人接受。《史记》记载《孟子》为七篇，而应劭《风俗通义·穷通篇》却说："退与万章之徒序《诗》《书》，仲尼之意，作书中、外十一篇。"《汉书·艺文志》也著录"《孟子》十一篇"。赵岐以《外书》四篇为伪，故不为之作注，后世研读者日少，逐渐亡佚。到了明代，姚士粦又伪撰《孟子外书》四篇，清人周广业指斥其"显属伪托"，梁启超则以其为"伪中出伪"。

《孟子》七篇，每篇分上下，计十四卷二百六十章，总计三万五千余字，是"四书"中部头最大、内容最丰富的一本。但长期以来《孟子》一直处于子书或传文位置，直到五代十国时期后蜀诏刻十一经将其列入，后宋太宗加以翻刻，《孟子》才开始进入经书行列。到南宋朱熹把《论语》《大学》《中庸》《孟子》合刊编写《四书章句集注》，《孟子》更加受到学者重视，孟子的思想也更大程度上影响了中国古代思想史的进程。

二、《孟子》之思想

　　《孟子》一书思想宏大、细致入微，主要反映了孟子本人及其同时代人的人性论、政治思想，以及孟子本人独特的经济思想、生态观、工夫论，其中涵盖了其与时人的义利（欲）之辩、人禽之辩、性命之辩、心体之辩等诸多内容。但由于其语录体的展开形式，孟子的同一思想多散落到各篇的许多章中，我们在理解的时候要仔细爬梳，把同一主题的全部相关内容放到一起进行综合判断，而不能一叶障目、断章取义。

　　人性论　人性论是先秦诸子乃至整个中国思想史的核心论题，孟子的人性论更是其思想体系的出发点和终极依据。孟子的人性论是通过其与告子的辩论展开的，主要见于《告子上》一篇。告子认为"性无善无不善"，其时还有人认为"性可以为善，可以为不善"，后来荀子则力主性恶论，与此相对，孟子的人性论为性善论。这些都是继孔子"性相近"之后的不同阐发路径。

孟子"性善论"之"性"是指人之异于禽兽的"几希"之性，而不是作为实然起点的与生俱来的性的全部；其"善"则是指道德意义上的正向发挥。孟子证明性善是通过心善来完成的，以心善言性善，即本心在摆脱生理欲望后自主呈现的善，是人之所以为人的道德主体，是性善的根本依据。所以其有涵盖恻隐之心、羞恶之心、恭敬之心、是非之心的"四心"说，并以此四心为仁、义、礼、智四德之端，由此说明"四心""四德"皆"非由外铄我也，我固有之也"。需要注意的是孟子并不认为四德是齐一的，而仍是以"仁"为统领的。既然性是善的，那恶又从何而来？孟子认为人受于耳目物欲之蔽而丧失其本心，恶由是而生。告子认为"食色性也"，但孟子认为耳目之欲一类虽从与生俱来意义上是为性的，而从其实现意义上则取决于外，是有命的，故人的本心是会被物欲所蔽而最终失于流放的，所以"君子不谓性也"。既然恶能产生，我们又当如何处理呢？

孟子提出"求其放心"的方法论。"放心"就是被物欲"引之"而流失的本心，若要回归本性之善，必须找回此"放心"，使其复如原态。此一过程全由人的自觉意识和自主行动主宰，所以孟子的性善论既是对人的价值的肯定，也推动了人主体自由的崛起和心灵自主的实现，正如其所说"万物皆备于我"，以及"舍我其谁"的自信精神。

性情关系是孟子人性论的又一重要论述，"乃若其情，则可以为善矣，乃所谓善也"，其意为情理并非经验，应然未必实然，价值根源于主体自觉，实现价值的能力就在性善的本质之中。孟子的人性论是和天命论相伴而行的，其内在逻辑为"尽其心者，知其性也；知其性，则知天矣"。由此而衍生出"存其心，养其性，所以事天也"的工夫论。

　　工夫论　孟子的工夫论可以概括为：存心、养性、集义、养浩然之气。存心、养性皆直接出自其性善论，前文已交代明白，此处，外加一条便是防范本心之失的根本措施——寡欲。

　　孟子极为注重集义，不仅与告子进行义内义外的辩论，而且直言"礼门义路"，把践行仁义作为人生唯一的根本正途。由集义而生养浩然之气，浩然之气至大至刚，就是"集义所生者"。人性是善的，但社会环境是复杂的，环境的复杂极易导致人性背离本善，所以人人皆需时刻自持。总之，孟子的工夫论就是保养其性善论的方法论，就是扩充四端的根本要求。

　　政治思想　孟子的政治思想是其思想体系的致用主体部分，也是先秦各家政治思想中的巅峰之作。如萧公权《中国政治思想史》所说："孟子之政治思想遂成为针对虐政之永久抗议。"孟子直接继承孔子"苛政猛于虎"

的批判，针对"民之憔悴于虐政"的现实情况，孟子把孔子仁的思想具体发展成为切于时弊的仁政思想。孟子仁政思想的巨大贡献在于其扭转了政治思想中的君民关系，把统治者为政治意志统领的位置转变为一切以人民的意志为根据，统治者遂沦为政治的执行者，而人民成为真正的政治归属，即民本思想。

孟子的"民为贵，社稷次之，君为轻"一语道破玄机，成为中国历代君王头上那把高悬的民意之剑。遵循民意也就成了统治者行事的根本出发点，必得以民"所欲与之聚之，所恶勿施尔也"，也就是《梁惠王下》中所说的"国人杀之"。如果统治者不以民意行事，甚至为国作乱、恣意施政，那该怎么处理呢？孟子对此提出了政权转移的学说。齐宣王以为"汤放桀，武王伐纣"是弑君行为，而孟子却说："贼仁者谓之贼，贼义者谓之残，残贼之人谓之一夫。闻诛一夫纣矣，未闻弑君也。"可见君之为君必得践行仁义，而不能戕害仁义、祸乱百姓，否则君便不再称其君，人人可取而代之。但此一政权转移说被历代统治者解释、执行为双重标准：一方面，在取代上一政权时，批判其违背民意而被自己取代；另一方面，到王朝后期，政治日渐腐败时，自己则对此说讳莫如深。基于此说，孟子在游说各国君主时，常常劝其施行仁政、招揽人心，此所谓"王道"（"王天下"之道）。

由仁政，孟子还提出了与之相关的具体措施，其中蕴含了与民养教、发展经济、保护生态等特色内容。"先王有不忍人之心，斯有不忍人之政矣"，王者要有"天下有溺者，由己溺之也……天下有饥者，由己饥之也"的同情之心，以及在此同情之心的基础上发展出"解民于倒悬"的"不忍人之政"。民众的幸福首先来自生活的富足，所以孟子提出"制民之产"，提出"五亩之宅，树之以桑""鸡豚狗彘之畜，无失其时""百亩之田，勿夺其时""谨庠序之教，申之以孝悌之义"的养教措施。只要统治者肯认真施行，则"黎民不饥不寒""民养生丧死无憾也"，进而民有所恒产，"有恒产者有恒心"，也就避免了"无恒产者无恒心。苟无恒心，放辟邪侈，无不为已"的混乱局面，如此也就不会"不王"了。

孟子的经济思想进而衍生出了生态保护的思想，即"数罟不入洿池""斧斤以时入山林"，虽然很难说孟子自主意识里保护自然的思想是成熟的，但这种朴素的主张确实有其重要历史意义。而且孟子经济思想中还兼顾农、工、商诸业。对于农业，他构建了理想化的"井田制"（无论井田制在孟子之前是否施行过，孟子提出的井田制都是一种土地改革意愿式的理想化主张）；对于工商业，他提出"关，市讥而不征""市，廛而不征，法而不廛"，使其自由发展而不设限。孟子的政治思想博大精深，在战国时期诸侯争霸的时代背景中可谓是一股清流，但其"贵王贱霸"的主张和诸侯国君的利益诉求背道而驰，常被认为是"迂远而阔于事情"，终未被接受和施行，而其在思想史上却具有深远意义，对后世为政者的警醒和对民众的养教也有着不可磨灭的历史贡献。

我们分析孟子思想体系时，尤需注意孟子的人文关怀、现实关怀，注意其以继承发扬孔子思想为己任的使命感，注意其发先圣所未发的创新点，注意其针对"邪说"加以批驳的责任感。其论说多有所指，而非是"好辩"而已。其说："杨墨之道不息，孔子之道不著，是邪说诬民，充塞仁义也。"

三、七篇贻矩，惠及今日

清雍正皇帝手书"七篇贻矩"金匾，悬挂于山东邹城孟府大堂檐下正中，向人们昭示着孟子著书的伟大功绩和对后世的惠及之恩。本书能将两千多年前孟子的著述再次呈现给读者，并把其中的思想价值进行现代化阐释，也是我们承担历史接续的光荣。

《孟子》的历史价值　孔子罕言性与命，到子思则大论性命，到了孟子更是把儒家性命论推向了高峰，所以学界有"思孟学派"一说。这一性命论不仅参与了先秦诸子的历史讨论，还直接影响了宋明以来程朱理学、陆王心学的此起彼伏。孟子的政治思想虽未能在当时施行，但其理论进步意义远高于当时指导兼并战争的"合纵连横"思想，而且孟子反对战争，认为"春秋无义战"。孟子的仁政思想其实不是简单的民本主义，其内在确实含有近代民主主义的色彩。自秦以降，中国历代都没能很好地执行孟子政治思想中最为根本的积极因素，甚至某些时候与之背道而驰，与孟子思想比照起来可以说是一种历史的倒退。孟子在其思想中呈现出的伟岸人格为历代读书人所景仰，孟子思想中的永恒意义一直照耀着我们前行的道路。

《孟子》的现实价值　孟子距今已两千

余载，但其思想时刻浮现在我们脑海，其教诲始终萦绕于我们耳边。继承孟子思想是我们的历史责任，发扬孟子哲学是我们的时代使命，所以我们必须深入理解孟子思想，解剖其实质内涵，辨析其根本，进而完成其创造性转化，通过实践使之得到创新性发展。回望身后，其实也照耀着前方的路。孟子思想体系中的积极因素，既有着进行历史研究、哲学研究、政治研究、社会研究的重大学术价值，也有着指导当下实践、启发政治生活、警醒不良之风的实际意义。而这些意义的实现前提是我们要立足当下，科学把握孟子思想，真正把《孟子》读好、读透。

Contents

滕文公上

5.1

　　滕文公为世子[1]，将之楚，过宋而见孟子。孟子道性善，言必称尧、舜。

　　世子自楚反，复见孟子。孟子曰："世子疑吾言乎？夫道一而已矣。成覸[2]谓齐景公曰：'彼丈夫也，我丈夫也，吾何畏彼哉？'颜渊曰："舜何人也？予何人也？有为者亦若是。'公明仪[3]曰："文王我师也，周公岂欺我哉？'今滕，绝长补短，将五十里也，犹可以为善国。《书》曰："若药不瞑眩[4]，厥疾不瘳[5]。'"

When the prince, afterwards duke Wen of Teng, had to go to Chu, he went by way of Song, and visited Mencius. Mencius discoursed to him how the nature of man is good, and when speaking, always made laudatory reference to Yao and Shun.

When the prince was returning from Chu,

he again visited Mencius. Mencius said to him, "Prince, do you doubt my words? The path is one, and only one. Cheng Gan said to duke Jing of Qi, 'They were men. I am a man. Why should I stand in awe of them?' Yan Yuan said, 'What kind of man was Shun? What kind of man am I? He who exerts himself will also become such as he was. ' Gongming Yi said, 'King Wen is my teacher. How should the duke of Zhou deceive me by those words?' Now, Teng, taking its length with its breadth, will amount, I suppose, to fifty *li*. It is small, but still sufficient to make a good State. It is said in the *Book of History*, 'If medicine do not raise a commotion in the patient, his disease will not be cured by it. ' "

【注释】［１］世子：王公诸侯的嗣子。［２］成 觋（jiàn）：齐国的勇士。［３］公明仪：鲁国 贤人，曾子的学生。［４］瞑眩：指用药之后 头晕目眩的反应。［５］瘳（chōu）：病愈。

【译文】滕文公还是太子的时候，到楚国去，途经宋国拜访了孟子。孟子给滕文公讲述人性本向善的道理，张口必称赞尧、舜。

太子从楚国回来途中，又去拜访孟子。孟子说："太子不相信我的话吗？道理都是一样的。成覸对齐景公说：'他是男子汉，我也是男子汉，我为什么要怕他呢？'颜渊回答说：'舜是什么人呢？我又是什么人呢？有所作为者都会像他那样的。'公明仪说：'文王是我老师，周公怎能会欺骗我？'如今的滕国，如果把疆土截长补短也将近方圆五十里了，尚且还可以治理成一个好国家。《尚书》中说：'如果药不能使人头晕目眩，病是不能痊愈的。'"

【解读】孟子主张性本善，认为人本性是向善的，未尝有恶，如果能够扩而充之，人人都可以成为尧、舜那样的人。"言必称尧、舜"，是孟子情感的真实反映，也是他的一种政治理想。本章孟子用成覸的"丈夫之勇"、颜子的"舜可为之心"、公明仪的"文王可师"来激励、叮咛滕文公，希望滕文公朝着尧、舜之道前行。而尧、舜圣贤之道，能否实现就在于"为"与"不为"之间。只要滕文公肯努力践行圣贤大道，滕国即便是小国，也可以成就大同。在孟子看来，滕文公是"不为也，非不能也"（《孟子·梁惠王上》）。只要自己相信并坚定地去做，圣贤并非高不可攀。

5.2

滕定公薨^[1]。世子谓然友^[2]曰："昔者孟子尝与我言于宋，于心终不忘。今也不幸至于大故^[3]，吾欲使子问于孟子，然后行事。"

然友之邹问于孟子。

孟子曰："不亦善乎！亲丧固所自尽^[4]也。曾子^[5]曰：'生，事之以礼；死，葬之以礼，祭之以礼，可谓孝矣。'诸侯之礼，吾未之学也；虽然，吾尝闻之矣。三年之丧，齐疏之服^[6]，饘粥^[7]之食，自天子达于庶人，三代共之。"

然友反命，定为三年之丧。父兄百官皆不欲，曰："吾宗国^[8]鲁先君莫之行，吾先君亦莫之行也，至于子之身而反之，不可。且《志》^[9]曰：'丧祭从先祖。'"曰："吾有所受之也。"

谓然友曰："吾他日未尝学问，好驰马试剑。今也父兄百官不我足也，恐其不能尽于大事，子为我问孟子。"

然友复之邹问孟子。

孟子曰："然。不可以他求者也。孔子曰：
'君薨，听于冢宰[10]。歠[11]粥，面深墨。
即位而哭，百官有司，莫敢不哀，先之也。'
上有好者，下必有甚焉者矣。'君子之德，风也；
小人之德，草也。草尚之风必偃[12]。'是在
世子。"

然友反命。

世子曰："然。是诚在我。"

五月居庐[13]，未有命戒。百官族人可，
谓曰知。及至葬，四方来观之，颜色之戚，
哭泣之哀，吊者大悦。

When the duke Ding of Teng died, the prince
said to Ran You, "Formerly, Mencius spoke with
me in Song, and in my mind I have never forgotten
his words. Now, alas! this great duty to my father
devolves upon me; I wish to send you to ask the

advice of Mencius, and then to proceed to its various services. "

Ran You accordingly proceeded to Zou, and consulted Mencius.

Mencius said, "Is this not good? In discharging the funeral duties to parents, men indeed feel constrained to do their utmost. The philosopher Zeng said, 'When parents are alive, they should be served according to propriety; when they are dead, they should be buried according to propriety; and they should be sacrificed to according to propriety;— this may be called filial piety.' The ceremonies to be observed by the princes I have not learned, but I have heard these points:—that the three years' mourning, the garment of coarse cloth with its lower edge even, and the eating of congee, were equally prescribed by the three dynasties, and binding on all, from the sovereign to the mass of the people. "

Ran You reported the execution of his

commission, and the prince determined that the three years' mourning should be observed. His aged relatives, and the body of the officers, did not wish that it should be so, and said, "The former princes of Lu, that kingdom which we honour, have, none of them, observed this practice, neither have any of our own former princes observed it. For you to act contrary to their example is not proper. Moreover, the *History* says, 'In the observances of mourning and sacrifice, ancestors are to be followed,' meaning that they received those things from a proper source to hand them down."

The prince said again to Ran You, "Hitherto, I have not given myself to the pursuit of learning, but have found my pleasure in horsemanship and sword-exercise, and now I don't come up to the wishes of my aged relatives and the officers. I am afraid I may not be able to discharge my duty in the great business that I have entered on; do you again consult

Mencius for me."

On this, Ran You went again to Zou, and consulted Mencius.

Mencius said, "It is so, but he may not seek a remedy in others, but only in himself. Confucius said, 'When a prince dies, his successor entrusts the administration to the prime minister. He sips the congee. His face is of a deep black. He approaches the place of mourning, and weeps. Of all the officers and inferior ministers there is not one who will presume not to join in the lamentation, he setting them this example. What the superior loves, his inferiors will be found to love exceedingly. The relation between superiors and inferiors is like that between the wind and grass. The grass must bend when the wind blows upon it.' The business depends on the prince."

Ran You returned with this answer to his commission.

The prince said, "It is so. The matter does indeed depend on me."

So for five months he dwelt in the shed, without issuing an order or a caution. All the officers and his relatives said, "He may be said to understand the ceremonies." When the time of interment arrived, they came from all quarters of the state to witness it. Those who had come from other states to condole with him, were greatly pleased with the deep dejection of his countenance and the mournfulness of his wailing and weeping.

【注释】［1］滕定公：滕文公的父亲。薨：死。古代称侯王之死叫"薨"。［2］然友：人名，太子的老师。［3］大故：重大的事故，指大丧、凶灾之类。［4］自尽：尽自己最大的心力。［5］曾子：曾子，名参（shēn），字子舆，春秋末年鲁国人，孔子的晚期弟子之一，儒家学派重要代表人物之一。［6］齐（zī）疏之服：

用粗布做成缝边的丧服。齐，指衣服缝边。古代丧服叫作衰（cuī），不缝衣边的叫"斩衰"，缝衣边的叫"齐衰"。［7］饘（zhān）：稠粥。粥：稀粥。［8］宗国：鲁、滕诸国的始封祖都是周文王的儿子，而周公封鲁，其行辈较长，所以其余姬姓诸国都以鲁为宗国。［9］《志》：记国家世系等的一种文书。［10］冢宰：官名。在君王居丧期间代理朝政。［11］歠（chuò）：饮。［12］偃，倒下。［13］五月居庐：居住在丧庐中五个月。

【译文】滕定公死后。太子对老师然友说："从前在宋国时孟子曾跟我交谈，我都牢记在心不忘。今天很不幸父亲去世了，我想请您先去请教孟子，然后再置办丧事。"

然友到邹国去请教孟子。

孟子说："再好不过了！父母的丧事本应该尽全力。曾子说：'父母在世，根据礼节侍奉他们；父母去世，根据礼节安葬他们，根据礼节祭奠他们，就可以称之为尽孝了。'诸侯的丧礼，我没有专门学习过。然而，我也曾听说过。守孝三年，穿粗布做的孝服，喝稀粥，从天子到平民百姓，夏、商、周三个朝代都是如此。"

然友回国复命，太子决定实行守孝三年的丧礼。滕国父老官吏皆不愿意，他们说："我们宗国鲁国的历代君主都未曾这样实行过，我们自己的历代祖先也没有这样实行过，到了您这里却违反规矩，这是不可以的。况且《志》上说：'丧礼祭祀都要根据祖先的规矩。'"他们又说："我们是有所依据的。"

太子对老师然友说："我以前没有做过什么学问，只喜欢驾车练剑。如今父老官吏们皆对我不满意，担心我不能处理好这件大事，请您再去替我请教一下孟子吧！"

然友又到邹国去请教孟子。

孟子说："是啊。不能改变也不能责怪别人。孔子曾说：'君王死了，冢宰代理政务。太子天天喝稀粥，脸色深黑而不梳洗。在孝子之位哭泣，大小官吏没有敢不悲哀的，关键在于太子要起到榜样的作用。'在上位的人有何喜好，下位的人就会喜欢得更厉害。君子的德行就像风，小人的德行就像草。草被风吹，必定会随着风的方向。因此，这件事完全取决于太子。"

然友回国复命。

太子说："是啊。这件事的确取决于我。"

于是太子在丧庐中住了五个月，未曾颁布任何命令和禁令。大小官吏和同族的人全部认可太子的做法，认为太子是知礼的。等到下葬的那天，四面八方的宾客都来观看，太子面容悲伤，哭泣哀痛，使前来吊丧的宾客都极为满意。

【解读】本章借滕定公之死，作为继承人的滕文公听从孟子建议，按礼法为父守丧尽孝，来说明当时孝道的丧失及民心从善如流的秉性。

"孝"在儒家思想中是基础性的概念范畴，由此扩充才得"忠"。滕文公要想得到百官及民众的认同，必须从"孝"入手，而为父守丧正是"孝"的一种重要体现。因此，滕文公听从了孟子的教诲，以身作则，"五月居庐"，被人称为"知礼"；及至葬，极尽哀泣，让人心悦诚服。另一方面，孟子提到"上有好者，下必有甚焉者矣""君子之德，风也；小人之德，草也。草尚之风必偃"，继承了《论语》学说，从中也体现出上位者对于下位者的示范、引导作用。历史上周文王施仁政，画地可为牢狱；齐宣王乐善言，举国争相进谏。越王喜勇士，臣子蹈火死；楚王好细腰，大臣扶墙起。上行下效是风吹草伏，至于吹何风，需慎之又慎。

5.3

　　滕文公问为国[1]。孟子曰："民事不可缓也。《诗》云：'昼尔于茅，宵尔索绹；亟其乘屋，其始播百谷。'民之为道也，有恒产者有恒心，无恒产者无恒心。苟无恒心，放辟邪侈，无不为已。及陷乎罪，然后从而刑之，是罔民也。焉有仁人在位，罔民而可为也？是故贤君必恭俭礼下，取于民有制。阳虎[2]曰：'为富不仁矣，为仁不富矣。'

　　"夏后氏五十而贡，殷人七十而助，周人百亩而彻，其实皆什一也。彻者，彻也；助者，藉也。龙子曰：'治地莫善于助，莫不善于贡。贡者校[3]数岁之中以为常。乐岁，粒米狼戾[4]，多取之而不为虐，则寡取之；凶年，粪其田而不足，则必取盈焉。为民父母，使民盻盻然[5]，将终岁勤动，不得以养其父母，又称贷而益之，使老稚转乎沟壑，恶在其为民父母也？'夫世禄，滕固行之矣。《诗》云：'雨我公田，遂及我私。'惟助为有公田。由此观之，虽周亦助也。

"设为庠序学校以教之：庠者，养也；校者，教也；序者，射也。夏曰校，殷曰序，周曰庠，学则三代共之，皆所以明人伦也。人伦明于上，小民亲于下。有王者起，必来取法，是为王者师也。《诗》云'周虽旧邦，其命惟新'，文王之谓也。子力行之，亦以新子之国。"

使毕战问井地。

孟子曰："子之君将行仁政，选择而使子，子必勉之！夫仁政，必自经界始。经界不正，井地不钧[6]，谷禄不平。是故暴君污吏必慢其经界。经界既正，分田制禄可坐而定也。

"夫滕壤地褊小[7]，将为君子焉，将为野人焉。无君子莫治野人；无野人莫养君子。请野九一而助，国中什一使自赋。卿以下必有圭田[8]，圭田五十亩。余夫二十五亩。死徙无出乡，乡田同井[9]。出入相友，守望[10]

相助，疾病相扶持，则百姓亲睦。方里而井，井九百亩，其中为公田。八家皆私百亩，同养公田。公事毕，然后敢治私事，所以别野人也。此其大略也。若夫润泽[11]之，则在君与子矣。"

The duke Wen of Teng asked Mencius about the proper way of governing a kingdom. Mencius said, "The business of the people may not be remissly attended to. It is said in the *Book of Poetry*, 'In the daylight go and gather the grass. And at night twist your ropes, then get up quickly on the roofs; —soon must we begin sowing again the grain.' The way of the people is this: —If they have a certain livelihood, they will have a fixed heart; if they have not a certain livelihood, they have not a fixed heart. If they have not a fixed heart, there is nothing which they will not do in the way of self-abandonment, of moral deflection, of depravity, and of wild license.

When they have thus been involved in crime, to follow them up and punish them: —this is to entrap the people. How can such a thing as entrapping the people be done under the rule of a benevolent man? Therefore, a ruler who is endowed with talents and virtue will be gravely complaisant and economical, showing a respectful politeness to his ministers, and taking from the people only in accordance with regulated limits. Yang Hu said, 'He who seeks to be rich will not be benevolent. He who wishes to be benevolent will not be rich.'

"The sovereign of the Xia dynasty enacted the fifty *mu* allotment, and the payment of a tax. The founder of the Yin enacted the seventy *mu* allotment, and the system of mutual aid. The founder of the Zhou enacted the hundred *mu* allotment, and the share system. In reality, what was paid in all these was a tithe. The share system means mutual division. The aid system means mutual dependence. Long said, 'For regulating the lands, there is no better system than that of mutual aid, and none which is not better than that of taxing. By the tax system, the regular amount was fixed by taking the average of several years. In good years, when the grain lies about in abundance, much might be taken without its being oppressive, and the actual exaction would be small. But in bad years, the produce being not sufficient to repay the manuring of the fields, this system still requires the taking of the full amount. When the parent of the people causes the people to wear looks of distress, and, after the whole year's toil, yet not to be able to nourish their parents, so that they proceed to borrowing to increase their means, till the old people and children are found lying in the ditches and water-channels—where, in such a case, is his parental relation to the people?' As to the system of hereditary salaries, that is already observed in Teng. It is said in the *Book of Poetry*,

'May the rain come down on our public field, And then upon our private fields!' It is only in the system of mutual aid that there is a public field, and from this passage we perceive that even in the Zhou dynasty this system has been recognised.

"Establish Xiang, Xu, Xue, and Xiao, —all those educational institutions, —for the instruction of the people. The name Xiang indicates nourishing as its object; Xiao, indicates teaching; and Xu indicates archery. By the Xia dynasty the name Xiao was used; by the Yin, that of Xu; and by the Zhou, that of Xiang. As to the Xue, they belonged to the three dynasties, and by that name. The object of them all is to illustrate the human relations. When those are thus illustrated by superiors, kindly feeling will prevail among the inferior people below. Should a real sovereign arise, he will certainly come and take an example from you; and thus you will be the teacher of the true sovereign. It is said in the *Book of Poetry*, 'Although Zhou was an old country, It received a new destiny.' That is said with reference to king Wen. Do you practise those things with vigour, and you also will by them make new your kingdom."

The duke afterwards sent Bi Zhan to consult Mencius about the nine-squares system of dividing the land.

Mencius said to him, "Since your prince, wishing to put in practice a benevolent government, has made choice of you and put you into this employment, you must exert yourself to the utmost. Now, the first thing towards a benevolent government must be to lay down the boundaries. If the boundaries be not defined correctly, the division of the land into squares will not be equal, and the produce available for salaries will not be evenly distributed. On this account, oppressive rulers and impure ministers are sure to neglect this defining of the boundaries. When the boundaries have been defined correctly, the division of the fields and the regulation of allowances may be determined by you, sitting at your ease.

"Although the territory of Teng is narrow and small, yet there must be in it men of a superior grade, and there must be in it country- men. If there were not men of a superior grade, there would be none to rule the countrymen. If there were not countrymen, there would be none to support the men of superior grade. I would ask you, in the remoter districts, observing the nine-squares division, to reserve one division to be cultivated on the system of mutual aid, and in the more central parts of the kingdom, to make the people pay for themselves a tenth part of their produce. From the highest officers down to the lowest, each one must have his holy field, consisting of fifty *mu*. Let the supernumerary males have their twenty-five *mu*. On occasions of death, or removal from one dwelling to another, there will be no quitting the district. In the fields of a district, those who belong to the same nine-squares render all friendly offices to one another in their going out and coming in, aid one another in keeping watch and ward, and sustain one another in sickness. Thus the people are brought to live in affection and harmony. A square *li* covers nine squares of land, which nine squares contain nine hundred *mu*. The central square is the public field, and eight families, each having its private hundred *mu*, cultivate in common the public field. And not till the public work is finished, may they presume to attend to their private affairs. This is the way by which the countrymen are distinguished from those of a superior grade. Those are the great outlines of the system. Happily to modify and adapt it depends on the prince and you."

【注释】［1］为国：治国之道。［2］阳虎：即

阳货，春秋时鲁国大臣季孙氏的家臣。［3］
校：比较。［4］狼戾（lì）：形容因为多而不
被珍惜。［5］盼盼然：愤恨而视的样子。［6］
井地不钧：井田划分不公平。［7］褊小：狭小。
［8］圭田：卿、大夫等人用于祭祀祖先的土地。
［9］同井：指处于同一块井田里。［10］守望：
指防范盗贼。［11］润泽：进一步加工。

【译文】滕文公向孟子请教治国之道。孟子回
答道："对待百姓的事是不能松懈的。《诗
经》上说：'白天去割茅草，晚上绞成绳索，
赶紧修缮房屋，到时播种庄稼。'百姓中有
这样一条准则，有固定产业的人就有相对坚
定的道德信念，没有固定产业的人就不会有
相对坚定的道德信念。如果没有坚定的道德
信念，那么违礼犯法、为非作歹的事，没有
不去干的了。等到他们陷入犯罪的泥沼，然
后便用刑罚处置他们，这就像是布下罗网陷
害百姓。哪有仁人做了国君却干陷害百姓的

事呢？所以贤明的国君必定要恭俭，以礼对待臣下，向百姓征收赋税有一定的制度。阳虎曾说：'要发财就顾不上仁爱，要仁爱就不能发财。'

"夏朝每五十亩地赋税采用'贡'法，商朝每七十亩地赋税采用'助'法，周朝每一百亩地赋税采用'彻'法，其实税率都是十分抽一。彻是'通'的意思，助是'借'的意思。龙子说：'管理土地，没有比助更好的，没有比贡更差的。'贡是比较若干年的收成，取平均数作为常数，按常数收税。在丰收年，粮食多得狼藉满地，多征些粮不算暴虐，相对来说征收得少；在灾荒之年，收获的粮食尚且不够下一年肥田的费用，税收却非要足额征收。国君是百姓的父母官，却使百姓一年到头劳累不堪，结果还不能养活父母，还得靠借贷来补足赋税，使得老人孩子流亡于沟壑之间，这样的国君哪能算是百姓的父母官呢？做官的人家世代享受俸禄的制度，滕国已经实行了。（何不再实行助法，让百姓也得到好处呢？）《诗经》上说："雨下到了我们的公田里，随即也下到了我们的私田里。"只有助法才有公田。由此看来，周朝实行的也是助法。

"要设立庠、序、学、校来教导百姓。庠，是教养的意思；校，是教导的意思；序，是习射的意思。地方学校，夏代称'校'，商代称'序'，周代称'庠'；'学'，夏、商、周三代都用这个名称，它们都是用来教人懂得伦理关系的。在上位的人明白了伦理关系，下位百姓自然就会相亲相爱。（如果这么做了）只要有贤明的国君出现，必然会效法，这样就成了贤明的国君的老师了。《诗经》上说：'岐周虽是古老的诸侯国，却新接受了天命。'这是讲的周文王。请大王努力施行仁政之道吧，以此来使您的国家气象一新。"

滕文公又派毕战来请教孟子井田的问题。

孟子道："您的国君打算施行仁政，所

滕文公问为国　韦辛夷　绘

以派您到我这里来，您一定要努力啊！施行仁政，一定要从划分和确定田界开始。如果田界不正，井田的面积就不均，作为俸禄的田租收入就不公平。因此暴君污吏必定要搞乱田地的界限。田界划分正确了，那么分配井田制定俸禄标准就可轻而易举地办妥了。

　　"滕国虽然地方狭小，但也要有人做官吏，也要有人做农夫。没有官吏就没有人来管理农夫；没有农夫就没有人来供养官吏。请考虑在乡野实行九分抽一的助法，在都市自行交纳十分抽一的赋税。卿以下的官吏一定要有可供祭祀用的五十亩土地，对家中还有剩余劳动力的，另给二十五亩。百姓丧葬迁居都不离乡，乡里土地在同一井田的各家，出入相互结伴，守卫防盗相互帮助，有病相互照顾，那么百姓之间就亲近和睦。一里见方的土地定为一方井田，每一井田九百亩地，中间一块是公田。八家都有一百亩私田，首先，共同耕作公田。公田的活干完后，才敢干私田里的活，这就是区分君子和农夫的办法。这是井田制的大概情况，至于如何改进完善，那就在于国君和您的努力了。"

【解读】本章滕文公问政于孟子，孟子从税制、学制、田制的角度具体论述自己的"仁政"思想，从中也体现出孟子的"民本"观念。孟子的一句"民事不可缓也"，足见对"民事"的关注。在胸怀仁爱的孟子看来，任何时代，任何社会，"有恒产者有恒心，无恒产者无恒心"，一旦百姓没有了恒产，成了无业游民，也就失去了基本的道德操守，什么胡作非为、违法乱纪的事情都能干得出来。所以要想社会稳定，首先要保障百姓的基本生存，农民有田耕，市民有工做，居者有其屋，只有家家有恒产，才能使得人人有恒心。而做到有恒产的关键就是税制与田制，实行合理的税制、田制，百姓才能够正常生活，官员才能得到供养。本章为我们了解我国历史上税制的发展，田制的价值，提供了史料。经济基础夯实了，方可去设立教学机构，去教化民众，使其明人伦之理，最终才可使社会长治久安，上层建筑才可稳固。孟子的这番话为社会问题的解决，提供了宏观上的路径。

5.4

　　有为神农之言[1]者许行[2]，自楚之滕，踵[3]门而告文公曰："远方之人闻君行仁政，愿受一廛而为氓[4]。"文公与之处，其徒数十人，皆衣褐，捆屦、织席以为食[5]。

　　陈良之徒陈相与其弟辛[6]，负耒耜而自宋之滕，曰："闻君行圣人之政，是亦圣人也，愿为圣人氓。"

　　陈相见许行而大悦，尽弃其学而学焉。

　　陈相见孟子，道许行之言曰："滕君，则诚贤君也；虽然，未闻道也。贤者与民并耕而食，饔飧[7]而治。今也滕有仓廪府库，则是厉[8]民而以自养也，恶得贤？"

　　孟子曰："许子必种粟而后食乎？"

　　曰："然。"

　　"许子必织布而后衣乎？"

　　曰："否。许子衣褐。"

　　"许子冠乎？"

曰："冠。"

曰："奚冠？"

曰："冠素。"

曰："自织之与？"

曰："否。以粟易之。"

曰："许子奚为不自织？"

曰："害于耕。"

曰："许子以釜甑爨，以铁耕乎^[9]？"

曰："然。"

"自为之与？"

曰："否。以粟易之。"

"以粟易械器者，不为厉陶冶；陶冶亦以其械器易粟者，岂为厉农夫哉？且许子何不为陶冶，舍^[10]皆取诸其宫中^[11]而用之？何为纷纷然与百工交易？何许子之不惮烦？"

曰："百工之事，固不可耕且为也。"

"然则治天下独可耕且为与？有大人^[12]之事，有小人之事。且一人之身，而百工之所为备。如必自为而后用之，是率天下而路^[13]

也。故曰：或劳心，或劳力；劳心者治人，劳力者治于人；治于人者食人，治人者食于人：天下之通义也。

"当尧之时，天下犹未平，洪水横流，泛滥于天下。草木畅茂，禽兽繁殖，五谷不登，禽兽逼人。兽蹄鸟迹之道，交于中国。尧独忧之，举舜而敷[14]治焉。舜使益掌火，益烈山泽而焚之，禽兽逃匿。禹疏九河，瀹济、漯[15]，而注诸海；决汝、汉，排淮、泗，而注之江，然后中国可得而食也。当是时也，禹八年于外，三过其门而不入，虽欲耕，得乎？

"后稷[16]教民稼穑，树艺[17]五谷，五谷熟而民人育。人之有道也，饱食、暖衣、逸居而无教，则近于禽兽。圣人有忧之，使契[18]为司徒，教以人伦：父子有亲，君臣有义，夫妇有别，长幼有序，朋友有信。放勋[19]曰：'劳之来之[20]，匡之直之，辅之翼之，使自得之，又从而振德之。'圣人之忧民如此，而暇耕乎？

"尧以不得舜为己忧，舜以不得禹、皋陶[21]为己忧。夫以百亩之不易[22]为己忧者，农夫也。分人以财谓之惠，教人以善谓之忠，为天下得人者谓之仁。是故以天下与人易，为天下得人难。孔子曰：'大哉尧之为君！惟天为大，惟尧则之，荡荡乎民无能名焉！君哉舜也！巍巍乎有天下而不与焉！'尧、舜之治天下，岂无所用其心哉？亦不用于耕耳。

"吾闻用夏变夷者，未闻变于夷者也。陈良，楚产也。悦周公、仲尼之道，北学于中国。北方之学者，未能或之先也。彼所谓豪杰之士也。子之兄弟事之数十年，师死而遂倍[23]之。昔者孔子没，三年之外，门人治任[24]将归，入揖于子贡，相向而哭，皆失声，然后归。子贡反，筑室于场，独居三年，然后归。他日，子夏、子张、子游以有若似圣人，欲以所事孔子事之，强曾子。曾子曰：'不可。江、汉以濯之，秋阳以暴[25]之，皓皓[26]乎不可尚已。'今也南蛮鴃[27]舌之人，非先王之道，子倍子之师而学之，亦异于曾子矣。吾闻出于幽谷迁于乔木者，未闻下乔木而入于幽谷者。《鲁颂》曰：'戎狄是膺，荆、舒是惩[28]。'周公方且膺之，子是之学，亦为不善变矣。"

"从许子之道，则市贾不贰[29]，国中无伪。虽使五尺[30]之童适市，莫之或欺。布帛长短同，则贾相若；麻缕丝絮轻重同，则贾相若；五谷多寡同，则贾相若；屦大小同，则贾相若。"

曰："夫物之不齐，物之情也；或相倍蓰[31]，或相什伯，或相千万。子比而同之，是乱天下也。巨屦小屦[32]同贾，人岂为之哉？从许子之道，相率而为伪者也，恶能治国家？"

There came from Chu to Teng one Xu Xing, who gave out that he acted according to the words of Shennong. Coming right to his gate, he addressed the duke Wen, saying, "A man of a distant region, I have heard that you, Prince, are practising a benevolent government, and I wish to receive a site for a house, and to become one of your people." The duke Wen gave him a dwelling place. His disciples, amounting to several tens, all wore clothes of haircloth, and made sandals of hemp and wove mats for a living.

At the same time, Chen Xiang, a disciple of Chen Liang, and his younger brother, Xin, with their plough-handles and shares on their backs, came from Song to Teng, saying, "We have heard that you, Prince, are putting into practice the government of the ancient sages, showing that you are likewise a sage. We wish to become the subjects of a sage."

When Chen Xiang saw Xu Xing, he was greatly pleased with him, and, abandoning entirely whatever he had learned, became his disciple.

Having an interview with Mencius, he related to him with approbation the words of Xu Xing to the following effect: — "The prince of Teng is indeed a worthy prince. He has not yet heard, however, the real doctrines of antiquity. Now, wise and able princes should cultivate the ground equally and along with their people, and eat the fruit of their labour. They should prepare their own meals, morning and evening, while at the same time they carry on their government. But now, the prince of Teng has his granaries, treasuries, and arsenals, which is an oppressing of the people to nourish himself. How can he be deemed a real worthy prince?"

Mencius said, "I suppose that Xu Xing sows grain and eats the produce. Is it not so?"

"It is so," was the answer.

"I suppose also he weaves cloth, and wears his own manufacture. Is it not so?"

"No. Xu wears clothes of haircloth.' "

"Does he wear a cap?"

"He wears a cap."

"What kind of cap?"

"A plain cap."

"Is it woven by himself?"

"No. He gets it in exchange for grain."

"Why does Xu not weave it himself?"

"That would injure his husbandry."

"Does Xu cook his food in boilers and earthenware pans, and does he plough with an iron share?"

"Yes."

"Does he make those articles himself?"

"No. He gets them in exchange for grain."

Mencius then said, "The getting those various articles in exchange for grain, is not oppressive to the potter and the founder, and the potter and the founder in their turn, in exchanging their various articles for grain, are not oppressive to the husbandman. How should such a thing be supposed? And moreover, why does not Xu act the potter and founder, supplying himself with the articles which he uses solely from his own establishment? Why does he go confusedly dealing and exchanging with the handicraftsmen? Why does he not spare himself so much trouble?"

Chen Xiang replied, "The business of the handicraftsman can by no means be carried on along with the business of husbandry."

Mencius resumed, "Then, is it the government of the kingdom which alone can be carried on along with the practice of husbandry? Great men have their proper business, and little men have their proper business. Moreover, in the case of any single individual, whatever articles he can require are ready to his hand, being produced by the various handicraftsmen: —if he must first make them for his own use, this way of doing would keep all the people running about upon the roads. Hence, there is the saying, 'Some labour with their minds, and some labour with their strength. Those who labour with their minds govern others; those who labour with their strength are governed by others. Those who are governed by others support them; those who govern others are supported by them.' This is a principle universally recognised.

"In the time of Yao, when the world had not yet been perfectly reduced to order, the vast waters, flowing out of their channels, made a universal inundation. Vegetation was luxuriant, and birds and beasts swarmed. The various kinds of grain could not be grown. The birds and beasts pressed upon men. The paths marked by the feet of beasts and prints of birds crossed one another throughout the Middle Kingdom. To Yao alone this caused anxious sorrow. He raised Shun to office, and measures to regulate the disorder were set forth. Shun committed to Yi the direction of the fire to be employed, and Yi set fire to, and consumed, the forests and vegetation on the mountains and in the marshes, so that the birds and beasts fled away to hide themselves. Yu separated the nine streams, cleared the courses of the Ji and Ta, and led them all to the sea. He opened a vent also for the Ru and Han, and regulated the course of the Huai and Si, so that they all flowed into the Jiang. When this was done, it became possible for the people of the Middle Kingdom to cultivate the ground and get food for themselves. During that time, Yu was eight years away from his home, and though he thrice passed the door of it, he did not enter. Although he had wished to cultivate the ground, could he have done so? The Minister of Agriculture taught the people to sow and reap, cultivating the five kinds of grain. When the five kinds of grain were brought to maturity, the people all obtained a subsistence. But men possess a moral nature; and if they are well fed, warmly clad, and comfortably lodged, without being taught at the same time, they become almost like the beasts. This was a subject of anxious solicitude to the sage Shun, and he appointed Xie to be the Minister of Instruction, to teach the relations of humanity: —how, between father and son, there should be affection; between sovereign and minister, righteousness; between husband and wife, attention to their separate functions; between old and young, a proper order; and between friends, fidelity. The high meritorious sovereign said to him, 'Encourage them; lead them on; rectify them; straighten them; help them; give them wings: —thus causing them to become possessors of themselves. Then follow this up by stimulating them, and conferring benefits on them.' When the sages were exercising their solicitude for the people in this way, had they leisure to cultivate the ground?

"What Yao felt giving him anxiety was the not getting Shun. What Shun felt giving him anxiety was the not getting Yu and Gaoyao. But he whose anxiety is about his hundred *mu* not being properly cultivated, is a mere husbandman. The imparting by a man to others of his wealth, is called 'kindness.' The teaching others what is good, is called 'the exercise of fidelity.' The finding a man who shall benefit the kingdom, is called 'benevolence.' Hence to give the throne to another man would be easy; to find a man who shall benefit the kingdom is difficult. Confucius said, 'Great indeed was Yao as a sovereign. It is only Heaven that is great, and only Yao corresponded to it. How vast was his virtue! The people could find no name for it. Princely indeed was Shun! How majestic was he, having possession of the kingdom, and yet seeming as if it were nothing to him!' In their governing the kingdom, were there no subjects on which Yao and Shun employed their minds? There were subjects, only they did not employ their minds on the cultivation of the ground.

"I have heard of men using the doctrines of our great land to change barbarians, but I have never yet heard of any being changed by barbarians. Chen Liang was a native of Chu. Pleased with the doctrines of Zhougong and Zhongni, he came northwards to the Middle Kingdom and studied them. Among the scholars of the northern regions, there was perhaps no one who excelled him. He was what you call a scholar of high and distinguished qualities. You and your brother followed him some tens of years, and when your master died, you forthwith turned away from him. Formerly, when Confucius died, after three years had elapsed, his disciples collected their baggage, and prepared to return to their several homes. But on entering to take their leave of Zigong, as they looked towards one another, they wailed, till they all lost their voices. After this they returned to their homes, but Zigong went back, and built a house for himself on the altar-ground, where he lived alone other three years, before he returned home. On another occasion, Zixia, Zizhang, and Ziyou, thinking that You Ruo resembled the sage, wished to render to him the same observances which they had rendered to Confucius. They tried to force the disciple Zeng to join with them, but he said, 'This may not be done. What has been washed in the waters of the Jiang and Han, and bleached in the autumn sun: —how glistening is it! Nothing can be added to it.' Now here is this shrike-tongued barbarian of the south, whose doctrines are not those of the ancient kings. You turn away from your master and become his disciple. Your conduct is different indeed from that of the philosopher Zeng. I have heard of birds leaving dark valleys to remove to lofty trees, but I have not heard of their descending from lofty trees to enter into dark valleys. In the *Praise-songs of Lu* it is said, 'He smote the barbarians of the west and the north, he punished Jing and Shu.' Thus Zhou-gong would be sure to smite them, and you become their disciple again; it appears that your change is not good."

Chen Xiang said, "If Xu's doctrines were followed, then there would not be two prices in the market, nor any deceit in the kingdom. If a boy of five cubits were sent to the market, no one would impose on him; linen and silk of the same length would be of the same price. So it would be with bundles of hemp and silk, being of the same weight; with the different kinds of grain, being the same in quantity; and with shoes which were of che same size." Mencius replied, "It is the nature of things to be of unequal quality. Some are twice, some five times, some ten times, some a hundred times, some a thousand times, some ten thousand times as valuable as others. If you reduce them all to the same standard, that must throw the kingdom into confusion. If large shoes and small shoes were of the same price, who would make them? For people to follow the doctrines of Xu, would be for them to lead one another on to practise deceit. How can they avail for the government of a state?"

【注释】 [1]为：这里指研究。神农之言：神农氏的学说。[2]许行：农家代表人物之一，生平不详。[3]踵：脚后跟，用作动词。踵门：指走到门前。[4]廛：一般百姓的住房。氓：移民。[5]衣褐，捆屦、织席以为食：穿粗麻衣，靠编草鞋、织草席谋生。衣（yì），动词，穿。褐，粗麻短衣。屦（jù），草鞋。[6]陈良：楚国的儒士。陈相、陈辛都是陈良的学生。[7]饔（yōng）：早餐。飧（sūn）：晚餐。[8]厉：病。[9]釜：金属制的锅。甑（zèng）：一种蒸饭的瓦器。爨（cuàn）：烧火做饭。铁：指用铁做的农具。[10]舍：相当于方言"啥"，即什么东西、一切东西的意思。[11]宫中：家中。古代住宅无论贵贱都可以叫"宫"，秦汉以后才专指帝王所居。[12]大人：这里指有地位的人，与下文"小人"相对。[13]路：指奔波、劳累。[14]敷：遍。[15]瀹（yuè）：疏导。济、漯（tà）：济水和漯水。[16]后稷：名弃，相传为周的始祖，尧帝时为农师。[17]树艺：种植。[18]契（xiè）：人名，殷人的祖先，相传是尧的臣子。[19]放勋：尧的称号。[20]劳之来之：劳、来都读为去声，劝勉，慰劳。[21]皋陶（gāo yáo）：人名，相传为虞舜时的司法官。[22]易：治。[23]倍：同"背"，背叛。[24]治任：准备行李。治，整治。任，负担。[25]秋阳：周历七八月，相当于夏历五六月，所以这里所说的秋阳实际相当于今天的夏阳。暴：同"曝"，晒。[26]皓皓：光明洁白的样子。[27]鴃（jué）：伯劳鸟。[28]戎狄是膺，荆、舒是惩：引自《诗经·鲁颂·閟宫》。膺，击退。惩，抵御。戎狄是北方的异族，荆、舒是南方的异族。［29］贾：通"价"。不贰：没有两样。［30］五尺：古代尺寸短，五尺约相当于现在三尺多一点。［31］倍：一倍。蓰（xǐ）：五倍。后文的什伯千万都是指倍数。［32］巨屦小屦：粗糙的草鞋与精致的草鞋。

【译文】有个奉行神农氏学说的人许行，从楚国来到滕国，觐见滕文公说："我这个从远方来的人听说您施行仁政，希望能得到一所住处，成为您的百姓。"滕文公给了他住处。他有门徒数十人，都穿着粗麻衣服，靠编草鞋、织席子谋生。

陈良的门徒陈相和他弟弟陈辛背着农具从宋国来到滕国，也觐见滕文公说："听说您施行圣人的政治，那您也是圣人了，我们愿意做圣人的百姓。"

陈相见到许行后非常高兴，完全抛弃了自己以前所学的而改学许行的学说。

陈相有一天去拜访孟子，转述许行的话

说："滕君的确是个贤明的君主，不过，他还没有掌握真正的治国之道。贤人应该和老百姓一起耕种，共同生活，一齐亲自做饭，治国理政。现在滕国却有储藏粮食的仓库，存放财物的仓库，这是损害老百姓来奉养自己，怎么能称得上贤明呢？"

孟子说："许先生一定要自己种庄稼才吃饭吗？"

陈相回答说："对。"

（孟子）问："许先生一定要自己织布然后才穿衣吗？"

答："不，许先生只穿粗麻衣服。"

（孟子）问："许先生戴帽子吗？"

答："戴。"

（孟子）问："戴什么帽子呢？"

答："戴生绢织成的帽子。"

（孟子）问："他自己织的吗？"

回答说："不是，是用粮食交换来的。"

（孟子）问："许先生为什么不自己织

呢？"

答："因为怕误了农活。"

（孟子）问："许先生用锅和甑做饭，用铁器耕种吗？"

答："是的。"

（孟子）问："他自己做的吗？"

答："不是，是用粮食交换的。"

（孟子）说："用粮食换取器具，无损于瓦匠铁匠；瓦匠和铁匠用器具换取粮食，难道就能够说是损害了农夫吗？而且，许先生为什么不自己烧窑冶铁做成各种农具，什么东西都放在家里随时取用呢？为什么要一件一件地去和各种工匠交换呢？为什么许先生这样不怕麻烦呢？"

（陈相）回答说："各种工匠的事情当然不是可以一边耕种一边同时干得了的。"

（孟子）问"那么治理国家就偏偏可以一边耕种一边治理了吗？官吏有官吏的事，百姓有百姓的事。况且，每一个人所需要的生活资料都要靠各种工匠的产品才能齐备。如果都一定要自己亲手做成才能使用，那就是率领天下的人疲于奔命。所以说，有的人从事脑力劳动，有的人从事体力劳动；脑力劳动者统治人，体力劳动者被人统治；被统治者养活别人，统治者靠别人养活：这是通行天下的道理。

"在唐尧的时候，天下还没有平定，洪水乱流，到处泛滥。草木生长茂盛，禽兽大量繁殖，五谷都不成熟，野兽威胁着民众。鸟兽经过的道路，遍布在中原地带。唐尧暗自为此担忧，选拔舜来治理。舜派益管火，益放大火焚烧山野沼泽地带的草木，野兽就逃避躲藏起来了。舜又派禹疏通九河，疏导济水、漯水，让它们流入海中；掘通汝水、汉水，疏通淮河、泗水的淤塞让水流入长江，这样一来中原地带才能够耕种并收获粮食。当这个时候，禹在外奔波八年，多次经过家门都没有进去，即使想要耕种，行吗？

"后稷教百姓耕种收获。栽培五谷，五谷成熟了才能够养育百姓。人之所以为人，吃饱了，穿暖了，住得安逸了，如果没有教养，那就和禽兽差不多。圣人又为此而担忧，派契做司徒，用人与人之间应有的伦常关系和道理来教育百姓：父子之间有骨肉之亲，君臣之间有礼义之道，夫妻之间有内外之别，老少之间有尊卑之序，朋友之间有诚信之德。尧说道：'慰劳他们、安抚他们、开导他们、纠正他们、辅助他们、保护他们，使他们各得其所，再进一步提高他们的品德。'圣人为老百姓考虑得如此，难道还有时间来亲自耕种吗？

"尧把得不到舜这样的人作为自己的忧虑，舜把得不到禹和皋陶这样的人作为自己的忧虑。那些把耕种不好田地作为自己忧虑的，是农夫。把钱财分给别人叫作惠，把好的道理教给别人叫作忠，替天下发现人才叫作仁。所以把天下让给人容易，替天下发现人才很难。孔子说：'尧做天子真是伟大！只有天最伟大，只有尧能够效法天，他的圣德无边无际，竟让老百姓找不到恰当的词语来赞美他！舜也是了不得的天子！虽然有了这样广阔的天下，自己却并不占有它！'尧和舜治理天下，难道不用心思吗？只不过不用在耕田种地上罢了。

"我只听说过用中原的一切来改变边远落后地区的，没有听说过用边远落后地区的一切来改变中原的。陈良本来是楚国人，却喜爱周公、孔子的学说，由南而北来到中原学习。北方的学者还没有人能够超过他。他可以称得上是豪杰之士了。你们兄弟跟随他学习几十年，他一死，你们就背叛了他。以前孔子死的时候，门徒们都为他守孝三年以后，大家才收拾行李准备回家。临走的时候，都去向子贡行礼告别，相对而哭，泣不成声，然后才离开。子贡又回到孔子的墓地重新筑屋，又独自守墓三年，然后才离开。后来，子夏、子张、子游认为有若（言谈举止）像孔子，（祭祀时）便想让有若扮演孔子，用尊敬孔子的礼来尊敬他，他们希望曾子也同意。曾子说：'不可以。老师的圣德就像用江汉的水洗涤过，又在夏天的太阳下曝晒过般洁白无瑕，是没有谁还能够相比的。'如今这个怪腔怪调的南方人，说话诽谤先王的圣贤之道，你们却背叛自己的老师而向他学习，这和曾子对先王之道的态度恰恰相反。我只听说过（鸟）从幽暗的山沟飞出来迁往高大树木的，从没听说过从高大的树木飞下来迁往幽暗的山沟的。《鲁颂》说：'攻击北方的戎狄，惩罚南方的荆、舒。'周公尚且要攻击楚国这样的南方人，你们却去向他学习，这简直是越变越坏了啊。"

陈相说："如果听从许先生的学说，市场价格就会统一，没有欺诈行为，即使打发一个小孩子去市场，也不会被欺骗。布匹丝绸的长短一样，价格也就一样；麻线丝绵的轻重一样，价格也就一样；五谷的多少一样，价格也就一样；鞋子的大小一样，价格也就一样。"

孟子说："各种东西的质量和价格不一样，这是很自然的，有的相差一倍五倍，有的相差十倍百倍，有的甚至相差千倍万倍。您想让它们完全一样，只是搞乱天下罢了。一双粗糙的鞋子与一双精致的鞋子价格完全一样，人们难道还会去做精致的吗？听从许先生的学说，是率领大家走向虚伪，怎么能够治理好国家呢？"

【解读】本章主要讲孟子所代表的儒家学派与农家学派进行的论辩。陈相投奔滕文公，安居乐业之后，放弃了儒家而改学农家，认同许行对于滕文公"未闻道也"的评价，也认为贤者、君主当与百姓同耕而食，自食其力。孟子"以子之矛，攻子之盾"，批驳陈相观点，同时提出了"劳心者治人，劳力者治于人；

治于人者食人，治人者食于人"的著名论断。劳心者的价值就是将天下治理好，劳力者农夫的价值就是将土地打理好，百工的价值就是将器械制造好，分工不同，相互配合、交换，才能构成一个有机的社会系统，才能保证社会这个系统的正常运行。没有分工的差别，人类如同倒退到野蛮的时代，只需要同吃同住，聚成团躲进山洞，防备野兽进攻。尧选拔了舜治理蛮荒的社会，舜派益管火焚烧山野沼泽地带的草木，又派禹疏通九河，后稷教百姓耕种五谷，尧又派契教育百姓应有的伦常关系，孟子认为尧舜的关注重点在于治理天下，而不在于耕种庄稼，这种非直接生产的工作本身也是一种劳动，所以他们的价值也是不能用耕田衡量的。此外，孟子又对陈相背弃师道、学习许行的行为从道德高度进行了批判。

于是，难堪又羞惭的陈相拿出一个论点，即奉行许行的做法，可使市场物价一致，能做到童叟无欺。然而陈相这一论断本身就存在漏洞——忽视了物品本身的价值与品质。孟子以此为突破口进行驳斥，认为许行的观点最终只能让人走向虚伪、欺诈。至此陈相之论，已无立足之地，只得哑口无言、全面败退。此处孟子"物之不齐，物之情也"的论断极为深刻，其意在"事物有价值差异，乃一种客观事实，强使不同者为同，即是制造混乱"（劳思光《新编中国哲学史》）。当然，我们也从本章窥视到农家的政治主张或者说古人的政治智慧，其积极意义主要表现在反对剥削，人人自食其力等。这些合理的成分在彼时有着很大的影响力，故而，陈相弃儒从农也在情理之中。

孟子的批判存在着或多或少的刻薄（如攻击陈相背叛师道），也存在着"夷夏之别"的局限性，但孟子敢于直言的浩然正气值得我们学习。

5.5

墨者夷之，因徐辟而求见孟子[1]。孟子曰：“吾固愿见，今吾尚病，病愈，我且往见，夷子不来！”

他日又求见孟子。孟子曰：“吾今则可以见矣。不直，则道不见[2]，我且直之。吾闻夷子墨者。墨之治丧也，以薄为其道也。夷子思以易天下，岂以为非是而不贵也？然而夷子葬其亲厚，则是以所贱事亲也。”

徐子以告夷子。

夷子曰：“儒者之道，古之人‘若保赤子’[3]，此言何谓也？之则以为爱无差等，施由亲始。”

徐子以告孟子。

孟子曰：“夫夷子，信以为人之亲其兄之子为若亲其邻之赤子乎？彼有取尔也。赤子匍匐将入井，非赤子之罪也。且天之生物也，使之一本，而夷子二本故也。盖上世尝有不葬其亲者。其亲死，则举而委之于壑。他日

过之，狐狸食之，蝇蚋姑嘬之[4]。其颡有泚[5]，
睨而不视。夫泚也，非为人泚，中心达于面目。
盖归反虆梩[6]而掩之。掩之诚是也，则孝子
仁人之掩其亲，亦必有道矣。"

徐子以告夷子。夷子怃然[7]为间曰："命[8]
之矣。"

The Mohist, Yi Zhi, sought, through Xu Pi,
to see Mencius. Mencius said, "I indeed wish to see
him, but at present I am still unwell. When I am
better, I will myself go and see him. He need not
come here again."

Next day, Yi Zhi again sought to see Mencius.
Mencius said, "Today I am able to see him. But if
I do not correct his errors, the true principles will
not be fully evident. Let me first correct him. I have
heard that this Yi is a Mohist. Now Mo considers
that in the regulation of funeral matters a spare
simplicity should be the rule. Yi thinks with Mo's

doctrines to change the customs of the kingdom; —
how does he regard them as if they were wrong,
and not honour them? Notwithstanding his views,
Yi buried his parents in a sumptuous manner, and
so he served them in the way which his doctrines
discountenance."

The disciple Xu informed Yi of these remarks.

Yi said, "Even according to the principles of
the learned, we find that the ancients acted towards
the people 'as if they were watching over an infant.'
What does this expression mean? To me it sounds
that we are to love all without difference of degree;
but the manifestation of love must begin with our
parents."

Xu reported this reply to Mencius, who said,
"Now, does Yi really think that a man's affection for
the child of his brother is merely like his affection for
the infant of a neighbour? What is to be approved
in that expression is simply this: —that if an infant

crawling about is likely to fall into a well, it is no crime in che infant. Moreover, Heaven gives birth to creatures in such a way that they have one root, and Yi makes them to have two roots. This is the cause of his error. And, in the most ancient times, there were some who did not inter their parents. When their parents died, they took them up and threw them into some water-channel. Afterwards, when passing by them, they saw foxes and wild-cats devouring them, and flies and gnats biting at them. The perspiration started out upon their foreheads, and they looked away, unable to bear the sight. It was not on account of other people that this perspiration flowed. The emotions of their hearts affected their faces and eyes, and instantly they went home, and came back with baskets and spades and covered the bodies. If the covering them thus was indeed right, you may see that the filial son and virtuous man, in interring in a handsome manner their parents, act according to a proper rule."

The disciple Xu informed Yi of what Mencius had said. Yi was thoughtful for a short time, and then said, "He has instructed me."

【注释】［1］墨者：信奉墨子学说的人。夷之：人名。徐辟：孟子的学生。［2］直：这里为正直、公正之意。见：同"现"。［3］赤子：指婴儿。［4］蝇蚋（ruì）：苍蝇和蚊子。喙（chuài）：叮咬。［5］颡（sǎng）：额头。泚（cǐ）：出汗的样子。［6］虆（léi）：土筐。梩（lí）：锹一类的器具。［7］怃然：指怅然失意的样子。［8］命：教。

【译文】墨家学派的信奉者夷之想通过孟子的学生徐辟求见孟子。孟子说："我是很愿意见他的，但我现在生病了，等病痊愈了我去见他，夷子就不用来了。"

过了一段时间，夷子又请求见孟子。孟

子说：“我现在可以见他。不直言以对，则
道理就会不显明，我姑且直言以对吧。我听
说夷子信奉墨家学说，墨家学说提倡置办丧
事，以节俭薄葬为正道；夷子想以此来移风
易俗于天下，难道认为不这样就不可贵了吗？
然而夷子又厚葬自己的父母，这就是用他认
为低贱的方法来对待父母了。”

徐辟把孟子的话告诉了夷子。

夷子说：“儒家的学说认为，古代帝王
对待百姓如同爱护婴儿一样，这是说的什么
意思呢？我认为意思是说爱是没有差别等级
的，只是施爱是由父母开始罢了。”

徐辟把夷子的话告诉了孟子。

孟子说：“这夷子真的认为人们爱护自
己哥哥的孩子与爱护邻居的孩子是无差别的
吗？那是有所取舍的。婴儿在地上爬着就要
掉进井里，并不是婴儿的过错。况且天下的
万物，每个都只有一个根本，但是夷子认为
有两个根本。大概上古之时曾经有不安葬自

己亲人的人，他的亲人死了，就把尸体扛到山沟里丢掉。以后又路过那里，他看见狐狸撕咬尸体，蚊蝇也都来叮咬。于是额头冒汗，斜眼不忍正视。这汗呀，不是流给别人看的，而是内心真情实感表现在脸上罢了。于是这人就返回去拿土筐和锹把尸体掩埋了。掩埋尸体诚然是对的，那么孝子和仁爱的人掩埋自己的亲人，自然也是有道理的。"

徐辟把孟子说的话告诉了夷子。夷子怅然若失地过了一会儿才说："他教导了我啊。"

【解读】本章是儒家"仁爱"与墨家"兼爱"展开的隔空之辩，针锋相对，充分显示了两家的思想差异。孟子指出，"爱无差等"是不符合人之常情的，不要说爱自己的孩子和爱别人的孩子不同，就是爱自己兄长的孩子和爱邻居家的孩子也是不一样的。一个婴儿将要爬进井里，人人都会施以援手，这是源于人人都有的恻隐之心，而并非无差别的爱。

那种没有差别的爱要么出现在生产感情的流水线上，要么就是生活在感情的真空里。相比之下，儒家的"仁爱"更具有实际操作性，更与人伦情理贴切。这种爱是以血缘关系为纽带，形成一个同心圆，先是爱自己的父母、兄弟，再到爱社会上其他人；再扩展到爱天地万物，爱大自然。这种爱不仅仅局限于自己的家人，而是一种推己及人的爱，是一种宽广、博大的爱。

至于丧葬问题，墨家主张薄葬，而夷子并没有按照自己的主张去做，厚葬了自己的父母，言行不一，显然是自相矛盾。《礼记·檀弓下》中孔子教导子路的一句话："敛首足形，还葬而无椁，称其财，斯之谓礼。"可见，儒家并非一味主张厚葬，而是强调礼葬，称其财而葬。像孟子葬其父是薄葬，葬其母是厚葬，就是因为前后的经济状况不同而已。

滕文公下

6.1

陈代 [1] 曰：“不见诸侯，宜若小 [2] 然；今一见之，大则以王，小则以霸。且《志》曰：‘枉尺而直寻’ [3]，宜若可为也。”

孟子曰：“昔齐景公田 [4]，招虞人 [5] 以旌，不至，将杀之。志士不忘 [6] 在沟壑，勇士不忘丧其元 [7]。孔子奚取焉？取非其招不往也。如不待其招而往，何哉？且夫枉尺而直寻者，以利言也。如以利，则枉寻直尺而利，亦可为与？昔者赵简子使王良与嬖奚乘 [8]，终日而不获一禽。嬖奚反命曰：‘天下之贱工也。’或以告王良。良曰：‘请复之。’强而后可，一朝而获十禽。嬖奚反命 [9] 曰：‘天下之良工也。’简子曰：‘我使掌与女乘。’谓王良。良不可，曰：‘吾为之范我驰驱，终日不获一；为之诡遇 [10]，一朝而获十。《诗》云：“不失其驰，舍矢如破 [11]。”我不贯 [12] 与小人乘，请辞。’御者且羞与射者比 [13]。比而得禽兽，虽若丘陵，弗为也。如枉道而从彼，何也？
且子过矣，枉己者，未有能直人者也。"

Chen Dai said to Mencius, "In not going to
wait upon any of the princes, you seem to me to be
standing on a small point. If now you were once
to wait upon them, the result might be so great
that you would make one of them sovereign, or, if
smaller, that you would make one of them chief of
all the other princes. Moreover, the *History* says,
'By bending only one cubit, you make eight cubits
straight.' It appears to me like a thing which might
be done."

Mencius said, "Formerly, the duke Jing of Qi,
once when he was hunting, called his forester to him
by a flag. The forester would not come, and the duke
was going to kill him. With reference to this incident,
Confucius said, 'The determined officer never
forgets that his end may be in a ditch or a stream;

the brave officer never forgets that he may lose his head.' What was it in the forester that Confucius thus approved? He approved his not going to the duke, when summoned by the article which was not appropriate to him. If one go to see the princes without waiting to be invited, what can be thought of him? Moreover, that sentence, 'By bending only one cubit, you make eight cubits straight,' is spoken with reference to the gain that may be got. If gain be the object, then, if it can be got by bending eight cubits to make one cubit straight, may we likewise do that? Formerly, the officer Zhao Jian made Wang Liang act as charioteer for his favourite Xi, when, in the course of a whole day, they did not get a single bird. The favourite Xi reported this result, saying, 'He is the poorest charioteer in the world.' Some one told this to Wang Liang, who said, 'I beg leave to try again.' By dint of pressing, this was accorded to him, when in one morning they got ten birds. The favourite, reporting this result, said, 'He is the best charioteer in the world.' Jian said, 'I will make him always drive your chariot for you.' When he told Wang Liang so, however, Liang refused, saying, 'I drove for him, strictly observing the proper rules for driving, and in the whole day he did not get one bird. I drove for him so as deceitfully to intercept the birds, and in one morning he got ten. It is said in the *Book of Poetry*: "There is no failure in the management of their horses; the arrows are discharged surely, like the blows of an ax. I am not accustomed to drive for a mean man. I beg leave to decline the office.' Thus this charioteer even was ashamed to bend improperly to the will of such an archer. Though, by bending to it, they would have caught birds and animals sufficient to form a hill, he would not do so. If I were to bend my principles and follow those princes, of what kind would my conduct be? And you are wrong. Never has a man who has bent himself been able to make others straight."

【注释】［1］陈代：孟子的学生。［2］宜若：似乎。小：小节。［3］枉尺而直寻：弯曲一尺而伸展八尺，比喻牺牲小的利益而换取大的成就。朱熹《四书章句集注》言："犹屈己一见诸侯，而可以致王霸，所屈者小，所伸者大也。"枉，弯曲。直，伸展。寻，古代长度单位，八尺为一寻。［4］田：打猎。［5］虞人：狩猎场的官吏。依礼制，君王召唤距自己较远的下属，要用相当的事物作为信物。"旌"用来召唤大夫，"弓"用来召唤士，召唤虞人，只能用皮冠。［6］不忘：这里指不怕。［7］元：首，指脑袋。［8］赵简子：晋国大夫。王良：春秋末年著名的善于驾车的人。嬖：人名，赵简子的幸臣。［9］反命：复命。反，同"返"。［10］诡遇：不按规范驾车。［11］不失其驰，舍矢如破：出自《诗经·小雅·车攻》。［12］贯：同"惯"，习惯。

[13] 比：合作。

【译文】陈代说："不去拜见诸侯，好像只是拘于小节吧；如今一去拜见诸侯，往大里说可以实行王道，使天下归服；往小里说可以在诸侯中称霸。况且《志》书上说：'弯曲一尺而伸展八尺。'似乎是可以如此以屈求伸。"

孟子说："以前齐景公去打猎，用旌旗来召唤看守猎场的官吏，那小官因旌旗的召唤礼节不对没有理睬，齐景公想把他杀了。有志之士不怕身处于沟壑的险境，有勇之士不怕被砍掉头颅。孔子会取哪一种呢？取不召唤就不去，如果不等召唤就上门而去，那是算作什么呢？况且弯曲一尺而伸展八尺的说法，是从利益方面考虑的。如果从利益方面考虑问题，弯曲八尺长而伸展一尺有利，是否也可以做呢？以前赵简子命王良为他的宠臣奚驾车打猎，整整一天都没有打到一只飞禽。奚回去就向赵简子禀告：‘王良真是天底下最不会驾车的人。’有人就把话告诉了王良。王良就对奚说：‘请让我们再去一次。’奚勉强同意后又去，一个早晨就打了十只飞禽。奚回去后又向赵简子禀告：‘王良真是天下最会驾车的人。’赵简子说：‘我让他专门给你驾车。’并告知于王良。王良不同意，说：‘我按规范为他驾车驰骋，终日不获一只飞禽；不按规范为他驾车，却一个早晨就能获得十只飞禽。《诗经》曾言：‘驱车驰马极熟练，放箭有如椎破物。’我不习惯为小人驾车，请不要任命。’驾车的人尚且羞耻于与奚这样的射手合作，即便合作能打到堆积如山的猎物，也是不做的。如果扭曲自己的志向而追随别人，那是为什么呢？并且你的想法错了，扭曲自己的志向，是不可能使别人正直的。”

【解读】此章孟子谈论士人的处世原则，即凡事要有其气节，不可"枉尺而直寻"。士人之仕，当知"气节"二字，明白做人的道理，知其有所为有所不为。"枉尺而直寻"固然有着变通的成分，但变通不能丧失原则和道义，苟且偷生的变通与孟子的人生观大相径庭。孟子主张的是"志士不忘在沟壑，勇士不忘丧其元"，这是士人的人生境界。陈代劝孟子为出仕可以"枉尺而直寻"，如同当年孔子陈蔡绝粮时子贡劝孔子"少贬焉"一样，核心在于一个"利"字，即士人为了出仕，为了逐利，为了实现所谓的个人价值可以将自己的志向、理想标准降低，这关乎做人的道德。孟子通过"虞人不往""王良不驾"两个故事对陈代的建议给予否定性回答。卑微如虞人、王良者，尚能抵挡住名利的诱惑，对不合礼仪的召唤、不合规矩的驾车敢于说不，更何况那些以天下为己任的士人呢？"枉尺"看似小节，实则关乎大义。于今天而言，就是告诫我们为人处事要讲原则，有道德底线，千万不要因蜗角虚名、蝇头微利而丧失了为人处世的气节。

6.2

景春^[1]曰："公孙衍、张仪^[2]岂不诚大丈夫哉? 一怒而诸侯惧，安居而天下熄^[3]。"

孟子曰："是焉得为大丈夫乎? 子未学礼乎? 丈夫之冠也，父命之^[4]；女子之嫁也，母命之，往送之门，戒之曰：'往之女^[5]家，必敬必戒，无违夫子!' 以顺为正者，妾妇之道也。居天下之广居，立天下之正位，行天下之大道^[6]。得志与民由之；不得志独行其道。富贵不能淫^[7]，贫贱不能移^[8]，威武不能屈^[9]。此之谓大丈夫。"

Jing Chun said to Mencius, "Are not Gongsun Yan and Zhang Yi really great men? Let them once be angry, and all the princes are afraid. Let them live quietly, and the flames of trouble are extinguished throughout the kingdom."

Mencius said, "How can such men be great

men? Have you not read the Ritual Usages? 'At the capping of a young man, his father admonishes him. At the marrying away of a young woman, her mother admonishes her, accompanying her to the door on her leaving, and cautioning her with these words, "You are going to your home. You must be respectful; you must be careful. Do not disobey your husband.' Thus, to look upon compliance as their correct course is the rule for women. To dwell in the wide house of the world, to stand in the correct seat of the world, and to walk in the great path of the world; when he obtains his desire for office, to practise his principles for the good of the people; and when that desire is disappointed, to practise them alone; to be above the power of riches and honours to make dissipated, of poverty and mean condition to make swerve from principle, and of power and force to make bend: —these characteristics constitute the great man."

富贵不能淫，贫贱不能移，威武不能屈　梁文博　绘

【注释】［1］景春：与孟子同时代的人，纵横家。［2］公孙衍：战国时期魏国人，纵横家，著名的说客。张仪：魏国人，纵横家主要代表之一，主张连横以服从秦国，与苏秦"合纵"相对。［3］熄：指战火平息，天下太平。［4］丈夫之冠也，父命之：古代男子到二十岁行加冠礼，表示成年，由父亲给予训导。［5］女：同"汝"，你。［6］广居：仁也。正位：礼也。大道：义也。（依朱熹《四书章句集注》）［7］淫：惑乱，迷惑。［8］移：改变，动摇。［9］屈：屈服。

【译文】景春说："公孙衍和张仪难道不是真正的大丈夫？他们发起怒来，诸侯们都会害怕。居家安静下来，天下就会平安无事。"

孟子说："这哪里能算是大丈夫呢？你没有学过礼吗？男子举行加冠礼的时候，父亲给予训导；女子出嫁的时候，母亲给予训导，送她到门口，告诫她说：'到了你丈夫家里，一定要恭敬谨慎，不要违背你的丈夫！'以顺从为原则，是为人妾妇应遵循的。（至于大丈夫，）则应该住在天下最宽广的住宅'仁'里，站在天下最正确的位置'礼'上，行走在天下最光明的大道'义'上。能实现理想时便与百姓一同前进；不能实现理想时便独自坚持自己的原则。富贵不能使他骄奢淫逸，贫贱不能使他操守动摇，威武不能使他意志屈服。这样才叫作大丈夫！"

【解读】本章的焦点在于讨论什么样的人可称为"大丈夫"。在景春看来，能够来往于诸侯国之间，并挑起战争的纵横家公孙衍、张仪，算得上是了不起的大丈夫，他们"一怒而诸侯惧，安居而天下熄"。但在孟子这里，"大丈夫"之大应在于大胸怀、大气度、大境界；在于其独立的人格、谨严的操守、高尚的气节。富贵不能使之迷乱，贫贱不能使之移志，威武不能使之屈服；本于仁，居于礼，行于义；

不媚俗，不阿世，不苟且；有原则，有底线，有法度方为孟子所赞誉的大丈夫。公孙衍、张仪之流当然不在此列，他们只不过是摇唇鼓舌、见机行事、奉行以顺从为原则"妾妇之道"的人物。尽管他们也做出了一番轰轰烈烈的业绩，但究其实质，是舍弃了正义，为了名利苟合取容于诸侯的枭雄，哪里称得上大丈夫？大丈夫实为一种理想的人格典范，有着"得志与民由之；不得志独行其道"的情怀。如今，我们皆应以大丈夫的标准衡量自己，砥砺自己，修养我们的身心，磨炼我们的意志，为中华民族的伟大复兴而努力奋斗。

6.3

周霄^[1]问曰："古之君子仕乎？"

孟子曰："仕。《传》曰：'孔子三月无君，则皇皇如^[2]也，出疆必载质。'公明仪曰：'古之人三月无君则吊^[3]。'"

"三月无君则吊，不以急乎？"

曰："士之失位也，犹诸侯之失国家也。《礼》曰：'诸侯耕助，以供粢盛^[4]；夫人蚕缫^[5]，以为衣服。牺牲不成^[6]，粢盛不洁，衣服不备，不敢以祭。惟士无田，则亦不祭。'牲杀、器皿、衣服不备，不敢以祭，则不敢以宴，亦不足吊乎？"

"出疆必载质，何也？"

曰："士之仕也，犹农夫之耕也，农夫岂为出疆舍其耒耜^[7]哉？"

曰："晋国亦仕国^[8]也，未尝闻仕如此其急。仕如此其急也，君子之难仕，何也？"

曰："丈夫生而愿为之有室，女子生而

愿为之有家。父母之心，人皆有之。不待父
母之命、媒妁之言，钻穴隙相窥，逾墙相从，
则父母国人皆贱之。古之人未尝不欲仕也，
又恶不由其道。不由其道而往者，与钻穴隙
之类也。"

Zhou Xiao asked Mencius, saying, "Did
superior men of old time take office?"

Mencius replied, "They did. The *Record* says,
'If Confucius was three months without being
employed by some ruler, he looked anxious and
unhappy. When he passed from the boundary of a
state, he was sure to carry with him his proper gift
of introduction.' Gongming Yi said, 'Among the
ancients, if an officer was three months unemployed
by a ruler, he was condoled with."

Xiao said, "Did not this condoling, on being
three months unemployed by a ruler, show a too
great urgency?"

Mencius answered, "The loss of his place to an officer is like the loss of his state to a prince. It is said in the *Book of Rites*, 'A prince ploughs himself, and is assisted by the people, to supply the millet for sacrifice. His wife keeps silkworms, and unwinds their cocoons, to make the garments for sacrifice.' If the victims be not perfect, the millet not pure, and the dress not complete, he does not presume to sacrifice. 'And the scholar who, out of office, has no holy field, in the same way, does not sacrifice. The victims for slaughter, the vessels, and the garments, not being all complete, he does not presume to sacrifice, and then neither may he dare to feel happy.' Is there not here sufficient ground also for condolence?"

Xiao again asked, "What was the meaning of Confucius's always carrying his proper gift of introduction with him, when he passed over the boundaries of the state where he had been?"

"An officer's being in office," was the reply, "is like the ploughing of a husbandman. Does a husbandman part with his plough, because he goes from one state to another?"

Xiao pursued, "The kingdom of Jin is one, as well as others, of official employments, but I have not heard of anyone being thus earnest about being in office. If there should be this urge, why does a superior man make any difficulty about taking it?"

Mencius answered, "When a son is born, what is desired for him is that he may have a wife; when a daughter is born, what is desired for her is that she may have a husband. This feeling of the parents is possessed by all men. If the young people, without waiting for the orders of their parents, and the arrangements of the go-betweens, shall bore holes to steal a sight of each other, or get over the wall to be with each other, then their parents and all other people will despise them. The ancients did indeed always desire to be in office, but they also hated being so by any improper way. To seek office by an improper way is of a class with young people's boring holes."

【注释】［1］周霄：魏国人。［2］皇皇如：若有所求而不得的样子。皇，通"惶"，为徘徊迟疑之意。［3］吊：慰问之意。［4］粢盛（zī chéng）：古代盛在祭器内以供祭祀的谷物。谷物有六：稻、黍、稷、粱、麦、菽，可以盛于器皿中的叫"粢"，已经盛于器皿中的叫"盛"。［5］缫（sāo）：把蚕茧浸在热水里抽丝。［6］成：肥壮。［7］耒耜（lěi sì）：古代一种翻地用的农具。［8］仕国：易于出仕的国家。

【译文】周霄问孟子："古代君子也会出来做官吗？"

孟子说："做官。有《传》说：'孔子

如果三个月没被君主任用便焦急不安，外出
他国一定给当地的君主带上礼品。'公明仪说：
'古时候的人三月内不被君主任用，就要去
安慰他。'"

"三个月以内不被君主任用就要安慰他，
是不是太急切了？"

孟子说："读书人失去了地位，就像诸
侯失去了自己的国家。《礼》说：'诸侯耕
田来供给祭祀物品，他们的夫人养蚕缫丝来
做祭祀的衣服。祭祀牲畜不肥壮，祭祀谷物
不干净，衣服不完备，是不敢来祭祀的。唯
有读书人没有田地，那么就可以不用祭祀。'
牲畜、器皿和衣服准备不充分，不敢来祭祀，
就更不敢置办宴会，这还不足以去慰问吗？"

（周霄又问：）"外出他国必须带上见面
的礼品，这是为什么？"

孟子说："读书人出来做官，就跟农夫
与耕地是一样的，农夫难道会因离开此地就
抛弃农具？"

（周霄说：）"晋国也是读书人可以做官的国家，但没有听说过为官有这么急迫的。为官如此急迫，君子却怕求官，是为什么？"

（孟子说：）"男孩生下来就希望为他寻到妻室，女孩生下来就希望为她找到夫家。父母的这种心情，人人都会有。但不等到有父母的许可，媒人的介绍，就钻洞偷看，翻墙约会，那么父母、国人都会瞧不起他们的。古时候的人并不是不想做官，而是讨厌不走正道求官。不走正道而做官的，就跟钻洞翻墙是一样的。"

【解读】士者，仕也。孟子认为，士这一阶层仿佛就是为做官而存在的，士人要做官犹如农夫要种地一样，有其天然的合理性和必然性。子路曾说"不仕无义""君子之仕也，行其义也"（《论语·微子》），要实现齐家、治国、平天下的理想，"仕"是士人的必由之途，是大义之举。孟子又强调说，做官固然重要，

91

固然急迫，"孔子三月无君，则皇皇如也"，但君子求官、做官要来得正当，走正道，否则是一种可耻的行为。"不由其道而往者，与钻穴隙之类也"，仕不由道，首先就丧失了士的独立人格和尊严，从而也丧失了士本身的价值。士与君，绝不是简单的依附关系，更不是俗套的买卖关系，士因义而依于君，君因义而结于士。义，才是士之出仕的大道。因此，我们应该明白，无论过去还是现在，做官只是我们实现人生理想的一种手段和方式，是我们服务于人民、服务于社会的一种途径。要做就做合乎道义的官，做明明白白的官，决不苟且，决不"钻穴隙"。

6.4

彭更[1]问曰:"后车数十乘,从者数百人,以传食[2]于诸侯,不以泰[3]乎?"

孟子曰:"非其道,则一箪食不可受于人;如其道,则舜受尧之天下,不以为泰。子以为泰乎?"

曰:"否。士无事而食,不可也。"

曰:"子不通功易事[4],以羡[5]补不足,则农有余粟,女有余布;子如通之,则梓匠轮舆[6]皆得食于子。于此有人焉,入则孝,出则悌,守先王之道,以待[7]后之学者,而不得食于子。子何尊梓匠轮舆而轻为仁义者哉?"

曰:"梓匠轮舆,其志将以求食也;君子之为道也,其志亦将以求食与?"

曰:"子何以其志为哉?其有功于子,可食而食之矣。且子食志乎?食功乎?"

曰:"食志。"

曰："有人于此，毁瓦画墁^[8]，其志将以求食也，则子食之乎？"

曰："否。"

曰："然则子非食志也，食功也。"

Peng Geng asked Mencius, saying, "Is it not an extravagant procedure to go from one prince to another and live upon them, followed by several tens of carriages, and attended by several hundred men?"

Mencius replied, "If there be not a proper ground for taking it, a single bamboo-cup of rice may not be received from a man. If there be such a proper ground, then Shun's receiving the kingdom from Yao is not to be considered excessive. Do you think it was excessive?"

Geng said, "No. But for a scholar performing no service to receive his support notwithstanding is improper."

Mencius answered, "If you do not have an

intercommunication of the productions of labour, and an interchange of men's services, so that one from his overplus may supply the deficiency of another, then husbandmen will have a superfluity of grain, and women will have a superfluity of cloth. If you have such an interchange, carpenters and carriage-wrights may all get their food from you. Here now is a man, who, at home, is filial, and abroad, respectful to his elders; who watches over the principles of the ancient kings, awaiting the rise of future learners: —and yet you will refuse to support him. How is it that you give honour to the carpenter and carriage-wright, and slight him who practises benevolence and righteousness?"

Peng Geng said, "The aim of the carpenter and carriage-wright is by their trades to seek for a living. Is it also the aim of the superior man in his practice of principles thereby to seek for a living?"

"What have you to do," returned Mencius,

"with his purpose? He is of service to you. He deserves to be supported, and should be supported. And let me ask, —Do you remunerate a man's intention, or do you remunerate his service?"

To this Kang replied, "I remunerate his intention."

Mencius said, "There is a man here, who breaks your tiles, and draws unsightly figures on your walls: —his purpose may be thereby to seek for his living, but will you indeed remunerate him?"

"No," said Geng.

Mencius then concluded, "That being the case, it is not the purpose which you remunerate, but the work done."

【注释】［1］彭更：孟子的学生。［2］传食：辗转受人供养。传，同"转"。［3］泰：通"太"，过分。［4］通功易事：不同行业相互交流成果，交换产品。［5］羡：多余。［6］

梓匠轮舆：《周礼·考工记》有梓人、匠人，为木工；有轮人（制车轮）、舆人（制车厢），为制车之工。［7］待：同"持"，扶持。［8］墁（màn）：本义为粉刷墙壁的工具，这里指在墙上乱画。

【译文】彭更问道："跟在身后的车几十辆，跟随的人员数百，在驿舍里吃遍了各诸侯国，不是太过分了吗？"

孟子说："如果是不合乎道义的，就是一篮子饭也不能够接受；如果是合乎道义的，就是像舜那样接受了尧的天下也不过分。你认为过分吗？"

（彭更）说："不。但读书人不劳动而白吃饭，是不可以的。"

（孟子）说："你不通晓用成果交换之事，用多余来补充不足，那么农民有了多余的粮食，妇女有了多余的布（就不知道如何交换）；你如果通晓这些事，那么木匠车工

们都可以从你那里得到吃的。比如说这里有
这么一个人，在家孝顺父母，出门尊敬长辈，
奉行先王的学说，以此来教育后辈求学的人，
却不能从你那里谋得食物。你怎么可以尊重
木匠车工们却轻视奉行仁义道德的人呢？"

（彭更）说："木匠车工，他们工作的
目的就是求得糊口；君子是为了修行道义，
其目的也是为了求饭吃吗？"

（孟子）说："你为什么以他们的目的
来看问题呢？只要他们有功于你，可以给他
们吃的就给他们吃罢了。况且，你是根据目
的给人饭吃呢，还是根据他们所做的功绩给
饭吃呢？"

（彭更）说："根据目的来决定是否给
饭吃。"

（孟子）说："比如这里有一个人，把
屋瓦打碎，在新刷好的墙壁上乱画，他的目
的就是借此来获得吃的，你给他吃的吗？"

（彭更）说："不。"

（孟子）说："那么你不是根据目的，而是根据功绩了。"

【解读】战国时代，诸侯争霸，风起云涌，各国君主纷纷招贤纳士，欲借重士人之力使国富民强，从而使国家立于不败之地。"士"作为一个特殊的阶层便应运而生。他们或本于致君王成为尧舜的使命，或出于拯万民于水火的责任，或为实现扬名于天下的抱负，游说诸侯，献言献策，指点江山，大展身手。他们虽然不事稼穑，却担负着敦行向善、教化万民的重责，可谓是国家社会的眼睛和良心，"传食于诸侯"本无可非议。但是，我们必须看到，在他们中间也不乏鸡鸣狗盗之徒，他们没有独立的人格和尊严，没有远大的理想和抱负，为了满足自身的名利需求苟合取容于诸侯。这些人其实不配为士，为食而仕已经缺失了一个士人的良心。正是基于这种状况，孟子方有"通功易事"之说，方有食志食功一问。传食于诸侯，应食之有道，食之有功。能够敦促君主遵循道义，施行仁政，就是食之有道；能够敦促君主放弃眼前的苟且，着眼于全局和长远，方为食之有功。于今而言，在我们向社会索取的时候，应该想想，到底做了什么"事"，我们又有何"功"。"彼君子兮，不素餐兮"（《诗经·伐檀》），我们可不能做那种尸位素餐只知索取不讲奉献的"君子"啊！

6.5

万章[1]问曰:"宋,小国也。今将行王政,齐、楚恶而伐之,则如之何?"

孟子曰:"汤居亳[2],与葛为邻,葛伯放而不祀。汤使人问之曰:'何为不祀?'曰:'无以供牺牲也。'汤使遗之牛羊。葛伯食之,又不以祀。汤又使人问之曰:'何为不祀?'曰:'无以供粢盛也。'汤使亳众往为之耕,老弱馈食。葛伯率其民,要[3]其有酒食黍稻者夺之,不授者杀之。有童子以黍肉饷,杀而夺之。《书》曰:'葛伯仇饷。'此之谓也。为其杀是童子而征之,四海之内皆曰:'非富天下也,为匹夫匹妇复仇也。''汤始征,自葛载[4]',十一征而无敌于天下。东面而征,西夷怨;南面而征,北狄怨,曰:'奚为后我?'民之望之,若大旱之望雨也。归市者弗止,芸者不变,诛其君,吊其民,如时雨降。民大悦。《书》曰:'徯我后,后来其无罚。''有攸不惟臣，东征，绥厥士女，匪厥玄黄，绍我周王见休 [5]，惟臣附于大邑周。'其君子实玄黄于匪以迎其君子，其小人箪食壶浆以迎其小人，救民于水火之中，取其残而已矣。《太誓》曰：'我武惟扬，侵于之疆，则取于残，杀伐用张 [6]，于汤有光 [7]。'不行王政云尔，苟行王政，四海之内皆举首而望之，欲以为君。齐楚虽大，何畏焉？"

Wan Zhang asked Mencius, saying, "Sung is a small state. Its ruler is now setting about to practise the true royal government, and Qi and Chu hate and attack him. What in this case is to be done?"

Mencius replied, "When Tang dwelt in Bo, he adjoined to the state of Ge, the chief of which was living in a dissolute state and neglecting his proper sacrifices. Tang sent messengers to inquire why he did not sacrifice. He replied, 'I have no means of supplying the necessary victims.' On this, Tang caused oxen and sheep to be sent to him, but he ate them, and still continued not to sacrifice. Tang again sent messengers to ask him the same question as before, when he replied, 'I have no means of obtaining the necessary millet.' On this, Tang sent the mass of the people of Bo to go and till the ground for him, while the old and feeble carried their food to them. The chief of Ge led his people to intercept those who were thus charged with wine, cooked rice, millet, and paddy, and took their stores from them, while they killed those who refused to give them up. There was a boy who had some millet and flesh for the labourers, who was thus slain and robbed. What is said in the *Book of History*, 'The chief of Ge behaved as an enemy to the provision-carriers,' has reference to this. Because of his murder of this boy, Tang proceeded to punish him. All within the four seas said, 'It is not because he desires the riches of the kingdom, but to avenge a common man and woman.' When Tang began his work of executing justice, he commenced with Ge, and though he made eleven punitive expeditions, he had not an enemy in the kingdom. When he pursued his work in the east, the rude tribes in the west murmured. So did those on the north, when he was engaged in the south. Their cry was 'Why does he make us last?' Thus, the people's longing for him was like their longing for rain in a time of great drought. The frequenters of the markets stopped not. Those engaged in weeding in the fields made no change in their operations. While he punished their rulers, he consoled the people. His progress was like the falling of opportune rain, and the people were delighted. It is said in the *Book of History*, 'We have waited for our prince. When our prince comes, we may escape from the punishments under which we suffer.' There being some who would not become the subjects of Zhou, king Wu proceeded to punish them on the east. He gave tranquillity to their people, who welcomed him with baskets full of their black and yellow silks, saying — 'From henceforth we shall serve the sovereign of our dynasty of Zhou, that we may be made happy by him.' So they joined themselves, as subjects, to the great city of Zhou. Thus, the men of station of Shang took baskets full of black and yellow silks to meet the men of station of Zhou, and the lower classes of the one met those of the other with baskets of rice and vessels of congee. Wu saved the people from the midst of fire and water, seizing only their oppressors, and destroying them. In the *Great Declaration* it is said, 'My power shall be put forth, and, invading the territories of Shang, I will seize the oppressor. I will put him to death to punish him, — so shall the greatness of my work appear, more glorious than that of Tang.' Song is not, as you say, practising true royal government, and so forth. If it were practising royal government, all within the four seas would be lifting up their heads, and looking for its prince, wishing to have him for their sovereign. Great as Qi and Chu are, what would there be to fear from them?"

【注释】［1］万章：孟子的弟子。［2］亳（bó）：在今河南商丘，即前人所谓的南亳。［3］要：通"邀"，拦截。［4］载：开始。［5］匪：同"篚"，装东西的筐子。玄黄：指献的丝帛。绍：继续。休：美好。［6］张：张大，即彰明正道。［7］有光：即更为辉煌。

【译文】万章问道："宋国，是个小国。现在要施行仁政，齐国、楚国感到憎恨而去讨伐它，怎么办呢？"

孟子说："成汤居住在亳地，与葛国相邻，葛伯放纵无道而不祭祀先祖。汤派人询问他说：'为什么不祭祀？'（葛伯）说：'没有牲畜来做祭祀用的牺牲。'汤派人送给他们牛羊。葛伯把牛羊吃了，还是不祭祀。汤又派人询问他说：'为什么不祭祀？'葛伯说：'没有谷物来做祭品。'汤派亳地的民众去为他耕田种地，给年老体弱的人赠送食物。葛伯却带领着他的民众拦住那些带有酒食米饭的人进行抢夺，不肯给的就杀死。有个孩童带着米饭和肉要赠送他们，却遭到杀害并被夺走了食物。《书》说：'葛伯与送饭者为仇。'就是指这件事。汤因葛伯杀死了这个孩童而去征讨他，四海之内的人都说：'这不是贪图天下的财富，是为平民百姓复仇。''成汤的征讨，从葛国开始'，先后征伐了十一个诸侯国而无人能够抵御。他向东征讨，西方各族的老百姓就埋怨；向南征讨，北方各族的老百姓就埋怨，都说：'为什么把我们放在后面啊？'民众对他的盼望犹如大旱时盼望下雨一样。他所到之处，赶集的不停止买卖，种田的不停止耕作，诛杀了残暴的君主，抚慰那里的民众，如同及时降下

的甘霖一样。民众非常喜悦。《书》说：'等
待我们的君王，他到来后就没有严刑峻法了。'
又说：'攸国不服，周武王就向东征讨，安
抚那里的男女，他们用筐装着黑色和黄色的
丝帛，以能够侍奉我们周王为荣，希望归服
了大邦周室。'那里的官吏把黑色和黄色的
丝帛装在筐里来迎接有德的官吏，那里的小
民用筐装着饭食、用壶盛着饮水来迎接周武
王的士兵。他们（商汤、周王）的做法是把
民众从水深火热中拯救出来，除掉了残暴的
君主罢了。《泰誓》说：'把我们的军队发
动起来，攻入他们的国土，除掉残暴的君主，
用杀伐来彰明正道，比成汤的功业还要辉煌。'
不施行王道仁政便罢，如果施行，四海之内
都会抬头盼望，要拥护这样的人来做君主。
齐国、楚国即使强大，有什么可怕的呢？"

【解读】"葛伯不祀"的故事颇耐人寻味。"不祀"
对上表现为不敬祖先，不法先王；对下表现

为不行仁政，不体民爱物，所以汤要帮助他施行仁政。送他牛羊，他把牛羊吃了，派人替他耕种赠食，他却不分善恶，甚至把送饭的孩子都杀了。葛伯不仁可谓至极！孔子说："仁远乎哉？我欲仁，斯仁至矣。"（《论语·述而》）仁者，人心也，"葛伯不祀"，非不能也，而不欲也，而不为也。孟子借葛伯的故事说明：施行王道仁政，不在于国家的大小强弱，关键在于一国君主的仁心和胆识。宋虽小国，欲行仁政，不行则已，仁政一行，必能做到"四海之内皆举首而望"，齐楚虽强，又何惧乎！况且，齐楚之所以宣言要征伐宋国，就是听说了宋欲行仁政，说是恶，实则惧。仁政强大到连齐楚这样的大国都害怕的地步，仁政之功可见一斑。本章给我们的启示：施行仁政，不在于国家的大小强弱，而在于施政者的仁心、决心、信心、勇气。

6.6

孟子谓戴不胜^[1]曰："子欲子之王之善
与？我明告子。有楚大夫于此，欲其子之齐
语也，则使齐人傅^[2]诸？使楚人傅诸？"

曰："使齐人傅之。"

曰："一齐人傅之，众楚人咻^[3]之，虽
日挞而求其齐也，不可得矣；引而置之庄岳^[4]
之间数年，虽日挞而求其楚，亦不可得矣。
子谓薛居州^[5]，善士也，使之居于王所。在
于王所者，长幼卑尊，皆薛居州也，王谁与
为不善？在王所者，长幼卑尊，皆非薛居州也，
王谁与为善？一薛居州，独如宋王何？"

Mencius said to Dai Busheng, "I see that you
are desiring your king to be virtuous, and will plainly
tell you how he may be made so. Suppose that there
is a great officer of Chu here, who wishes his son to
learn the speech of Qi. Will he in that case employ a

man of Qi as his tutor, or a man of Chu?"

"He will employ a man of Qi to teach him," said Busheng.

Mencius went on, "If but one man of Qi be teaching him, and there be a multitude of men of Chu continually shouting out about him, although his father beat him every day, wishing him to learn the speech of Qi, it will be impossible for him to do so. But in the same way, if he were to be taken and placed for several years in Zhuang or Yue, though his father should beat him, wishing him to speak the language of Chu, it would be impossible for him to do so. You supposed that Xue Juzhou was a scholar of virtue, and you have got him placed in attendance on the king. Suppose that all in attendance on the king, old and young, high and low, were Xue Juzhous, whom would the king have to do evil with? And suppose that all in attendance on the king, old and young, high and low, are not Xue Juzhous, whom will the king gave to do good with? What can one Xue Juzhou do alone for the king of Song?"

【注释】[1]戴不胜：宋国大臣。[2]傅：教。[3]咻（xiū）：喧扰。[4]庄岳：齐国的街里名。[5]薛居州：人名，宋国之臣。

【译文】孟子对戴不胜说："你想要你的国君向善吗？我明确地告诉你。假如有位楚国的大夫在这里，想要他的儿子能说齐语，是让齐人来教他呢，还是让楚人来教他？"

（戴不胜）说："让齐人来教他。"

（孟子）说："一个齐人教他，许多楚人在旁喧哗骚扰，即使每天责打要他说齐语，也不可能做到；要是带他到齐国的闹市里住上几年，即使每天责打要他说楚语，也不可能做到。你说薛居州是善士，要让他住在王宫里。如果住在王宫里的人，无论年纪大小、地位高低，都是薛居州那样的人，国君和谁去做不善的事呢？如果住在王宫里的人，无论年纪大小、地位高低，都不是薛居州那样的人，国君和谁去做善事呢？一个薛居州，怎能独自改变得了宋国国君呢？"

【解读】无论学习、工作还是生活，人文环境都是一个重要的客观因素。孟子对此是有切身体会的。"昔孟母，择邻处"（《三字经》），为了让孟子有一个良好的学习生活环境，孟母多次搬迁，择邻而处。孟子后天的成就与他早期良好的人文环境是分不开的。晋朝哲人傅玄在《太子少傅箴》中指出："近朱者赤，近墨者黑。"荀子曾言："蓬生麻中，不扶而直；白沙在涅，与之俱黑。"（《荀子·劝学》）可见环境对人的影响可谓大矣，很少有人能完全摆脱环境的干扰和束缚。"一傅众咻"的故事也从反面说明了这个道理。一人教，敌不过众人扰；同样，一人仁，也敌不过众人恶。行仁政，不仅取决于一国之君的仁心和决心，还取决于国君手下有一批与之同心同德、矢志不渝的大臣。君仁臣忠，心往一处想，劲往一处使，方能把政事处理好，方能取信于民。

6.7

公孙丑问曰："不见诸侯何义？"

孟子曰："古者不为臣不见。段干木逾垣而辟之[1]，泄柳闭门而不内[2]，是皆已甚[3]。迫，斯可以见矣。阳货[4]欲见孔子而恶无礼，大夫有赐于士，不得受于其家，则往拜其门。阳货瞰[5]孔子之亡也，而馈孔子蒸豚；孔子亦瞰其亡也，而往拜之。当是时，阳货先，岂得不见？曾子曰：'胁肩谄笑，病于夏畦[6]。'子路曰：'未同而言，观其色赧赧然，非由[7]之所知也。'由是观之，则君子之所养可知已矣。"

Gongsun Chou asked Mencius, saying, "What is the point of righteousness involved in your not going to see the princes?"

Mencius replied, "Among the ancients, if one had not seen a minister in a state, he did not go to see the sovereign. Duan Gan Mu leaped over his wall to avoid the prince. Xie Liu shut his door, and would not admit the prince. These two, however, carried their scrupulosity to excess. When a prince is urgent, it is not improper to see him. Yang Huo wished to get Confucius to go to see him, but disliked doing so by any want of propriety. As it is the rule, therefore, that when a great officer sends a gift to a scholar, if the latter be not at home to receive it, he must go to the officer's to pay his respects, Yang Huo watched when Confucius was out, and sent him a roasted pig. Confucius, in his turn, watched when Huo was out, and went to pay his respects to him. At that time, Yang Huo had taken the initiative — how could Confucius decline going to see him? Zengzi said, 'They who shrug up their shoulders, and laugh in a flattering way, toil harder than the summer labourer in the fields.' Zi Lu said, 'There are those who talk with people with whom they have no great community of feeling. If you look at their countenances, they are full of blushes. I do not desire to know such persons.' By considering these remarks, the spirit which the superior man nourishes may be known."

【注释】［1］段干木：晋国人，清高而不屑为官。魏文侯去拜访他，他却翻墙逃走不见。辟：同"避"。［2］泄柳：人名，鲁穆公时人。内：同"纳"，这里为接纳之意。［3］是皆已甚：这都太过分了。［4］阳货：鲁国大夫。［5］瞰（kàn）：窥视。［6］胁肩谄笑，病于夏畦：胁肩，耸起肩膀，装作恭敬的样子。胁肩谄笑形容逢迎谄媚的丑态。畦，本指菜地间划分的行列，这里作动词用，指在菜地里劳动。［7］由：指子路。

【译文】公孙丑问道："不拜见诸侯是什么道理？"

孟子说："古时不是君臣关系就不拜见。
段干木翻墙逃避魏文侯，泄柳关门不接待鲁
穆公，都太过分了。如情况迫切，是可以拜
见的。阳货想要孔子来见他，又厌恶别人认
为他无礼，大夫赠送东西给士人，士人如果
不能在家亲自接受，就应去大夫门下拜谢。
阳货探知孔子不在家时送给他蒸乳猪；孔子
也探知阳货不在家时前往拜谢。在那时，如
果阳货拜访在先，孔子怎么会失礼而不去拜
见他呢？曾子说：'耸肩对别人做出毕恭毕
敬的样子，强装出讨好的笑容，比夏天浇菜
地还痛苦。'子路说：'内心并不相投却要
去交谈，看他那脸色难看的样子，这种人不
是我能够理解的。'从这些话来看，君子应
该有何修养，就可以知道了。"

　　【解读】公孙丑所问见不见诸侯这一小问题，
实则关乎君臣之大义、士人之大节。士之可
贵，就在于其独立的人格、坚贞的操守，就

在于其始终都能循礼守道、知耻明义。孔子说："非其鬼而祭之，谄也。"（《论语·为政》）不是自己的祖先却跑去祭祀，这就是谄媚。同样，不是诸侯国国君的臣子，却主动跑去见国君这也逾越了古代礼法。其关键不在于见与不见，而在于因何而见，怎样去见，孟子在此就列举了阳货与孔子避而不见的实例。如果去见诸侯合乎道义，所见不悖于礼法，那何必死守教条而不见？但所见悖于礼法，不合道义就另当别论了。或为蝇营狗苟，或为改换门庭，为一己之私利去见别国诸侯，这种行为是应当为世人唾弃的。今天我们应该明白，无论何时，作为社会的良心，士人追求权势和地位，实现个人价值，见君要有道，要合礼，要维护自己的人格与尊严。德不卑于位，道不屈于势，无论何时，士都不能低下自己高贵的头颅，都不能做那种逢迎权势、有辱士节的事。

6.8

戴盈之 [1] 曰：“什一 [2]，去关市之征，今兹 [3] 未能。请轻之，以待来年，然后已，何如？”

孟子曰：“今有人日攘 [4] 其邻之鸡者，或告之曰：‘是非君子之道。’曰：‘请损 [5] 之，月攘一鸡，以待来年，然后已。’如知其非义，斯速已矣，何待来年。”

Dai Yingzhi said to Mencius, "I am not able at present and immediately to do with the levying of a tithe only, and abolishing the duties charged at the passes and in the markets. With your leave I will lighten, however, both the tax and the duties, until next year, and will then make an end of them. What do you think of such a course?"

Mencius said, "Here is a man, who every day appropriates some of his neighbour's strayed fowls.

Some one says to him. 'Such is not the way of a good man;' and he replies, 'With your leave I will diminish my appropriations, and will take only one fowl a month, until next year, when I will make an end of the practice.' If you know that the thing is unrighteous, then use all despatch in putting an end to it: —why wait till next year?' "

【注释】 [1] 戴盈之：宋国大夫。 [2] 什一：十分之一的税率。 [3] 兹：年。 [4] 攘：偷。 [5] 损：减少。

【译文】 戴盈之说："田租十分取一，取消关卡市场的税收，今年还办不到。先减轻征收，等到明年，然后再完全改正，怎么样？"

孟子说："现在有个人每天偷他邻居的鸡，有人对他说：'这不是君子的行为。'那人说：'我先少偷些，每月偷一只，等到明年，然后再完全改正。'如果知道这样做不符合正道，就赶快改正，为什么要等到明年？"

【解读】本章孟子用偷鸡之喻批评了戴盈之的懒政，甚是妙矣！其一，孟子鞭辟入里，一针见血地抨击了当政者的虚伪。所谓"偷鸡"者，聚敛于民，与民争利，虽然嘴上喊着要实施仁政，实际上却迟迟不肯立即改正。其二，"日攘一鸡"到"月攘一鸡"，少则少矣，但其实是五十步笑百步，"偷"民、虐民的实质并未改变，这一政策的制定往往是愚民而已。其三，揭露了统治者的伪善，指出了"除恶必速"的道理。宋国一面宣言要行仁政，一面又一拖再拖，甚至连十税一这样小小的仁政举措都拖而不决，让人不得不怀疑其仁政决心。

6.9

公都子[1]曰："外人皆称夫子好辩，敢问何也？"

孟子曰："予岂好辩哉？予不得已也。天下之生久矣，一治一乱。当尧之时，水逆行，泛滥于中国。蛇龙居之，民无所定。下者为巢，上者为营窟[2]。《书》曰：'洚水警余。'洚水者，洪水也。使禹治之，禹掘地而注之海，驱蛇龙而放之菹[3]。水由地中行，江、淮、河、汉是也。险阻既远，鸟兽之害人者消，然后人得平土而居之。

"尧、舜既没，圣人之道衰。暴君代作[4]，坏宫室以为污池，民无所安息；弃田以为园囿，使民不得衣食。邪说暴行又作，园囿、污池、沛泽多而禽兽至。及纣之身，天下又大乱。周公相武王，诛纣伐奄，三年讨其君，驱飞廉于海隅[5]而戮之。灭国者五十，驱虎、豹、犀、象而远之。天下大悦。《书》曰：'丕

显哉，文王谟！丕承哉，武王烈！佑启我后人，咸以正无缺。'

"世衰道微，邪说暴行有作，臣弑其君者有之，子弑其父者有之。孔子惧，作《春秋》。《春秋》，天子之事也。是故孔子曰：'知我者其惟《春秋》乎！罪我者其惟《春秋》乎！'

"圣王不作，诸侯放恣[6]，处士横议[7]，杨朱、墨翟之言盈天下。天下之言，不归杨，则归墨。杨氏为我，是无君也；墨氏兼爱，是无父也。无父无君，是禽兽也。公明仪曰：'庖有肥肉，厩有肥马，民有饥色，野有饿莩，此率兽而食人也。'杨墨之道不息，孔子之道不著，是邪说诬民，充塞仁义也。仁义充塞，则率兽食人，人将相食。吾为此惧，闲[8]先圣之道，距[9]杨墨，放[10]淫辞，邪说者不得作。作于其心，害于其事；作于其事，害于其政。圣人复起，不易吾言矣。

"昔者禹抑洪水而天下平，周公兼夷狄

驱猛兽而百姓宁，孔子成《春秋》而乱臣贼子惧。《诗》云："戎狄是膺，荆、舒是惩，则莫我敢承 [11]。'无父无君，是周公所膺也。我亦欲正人心，息邪说，距诐行 [12]，放淫辞，以承三圣者。岂好辩哉？予不得已也。能言距杨、墨者，圣人之徒也。"

The disciple Gongdu said to Mencius, "Master, the people beyond our school all speak of you as being fond of disputing. I venture to ask whether it be so."

Mencius replied, "Indeed, I am not fond of disputing, but I am compelled to do it. A long time has elapsed since this world of men received its being, and there has been along its history now a period of good order, and now a period of confusion. In the time of Yao, the waters, flowing out of their channels, inundated the Middle Kingdom. Snakes and dragons occupied it, and the people had no place where they could settle themselves. In the low grounds they made nests for themselves on the trees or raised platforms, and in the high grounds they made caves. It is said in the *Book of History*, 'The waters in their wild course warned me.' Those 'waters in their wild course' were the waters of the great inundation. Shun employed Yu to reduce the waters to order. Yu dug open their obstructed channels, and conducted them to the sea. He drove away the snakes and dragons, and forced them into the grassy marshes. On this, the waters pursued their course through the country, even the waters of the Jiang, the Huai, the He, and the Han, and the dangers and obstructions which they had occasioned were removed. The birds and beasts which had injured the people also disappeared, and after this men found the plains available for them, and occupied them.

"After the death of Yao and Shun, the principles

that mark sages fell into decay. Oppressive sovereigns arose one after another, who pulled down houses to make ponds and lakes, so that the people knew not where they could rest in quiet; they threw fields out of cultivation to form gardens and parks, so that the people could not get clothes and food. Afterwards, corrupt speakings and oppressive deeds became more rife; gardens and parks, ponds and lakes, thickets and marshes became more numerous, and birds and beasts swarmed. By the time of the tyrant Zhou, the kingdom was again in a state of great confusion. Zhou Gong assisted king Wu, and destroyed Zhou. He smote Yan, and after three years put its sovereign to death. He drove Feilian to a corner by the sea, and slew him. The states which he extinguished amounted to fifty. He drove far away also the tigers, leopards, rhinoceroses, and elephants; —and all the people were greatly delighted. It is said in the *Book of History*, 'Great and splendid were the plans of king Wen! Greatly were they carried out by the energy of king Wu! They are for the assistance and instruction of us who are of an after day. They are all in principle correct, and deficient in nothing.'

"Again the world fell into decay, and principles faded away. Perverse speakings and oppressive deeds waxed rife again. There were instances of ministers who murdered their sovereigns, and of sons who murdered their fathers. Confucius was afraid, and made the *Spring and Autumn*. What the *Spring and Autumn* contains are matters proper to the sovereign. On this account Confucius said, 'Yes! It is the *Spring and Autumn* which will make men know me, and it is the *Spring and Autumn* which will make men condemn me.'

"Once more, sage sovereigns cease to arise, and the princes of the states give the reins to their lusts. Unemployed scholars indulge in unreasonable discussions. The words of Yang Zhu and Mo Di fill the country. If you listen to people's discourses throughout it, you will find that they have adopted the views either of Yang or of Mo. Now, Yang's principle is— 'each one for himself,' which does not acknowledge the claims of the sovereign. Mo's principle is— 'to love all equally,' which does not acknowledge the peculiar affection due to a father. But to acknowledge neither king nor father is to be in the state of a beast. Gongming Yi said, 'In their kitchens, there is fat meat. In their stables, there are fat horses. But their people have the look of hunger, and on the wilds there are those who have died of famine. This is leading on beasts to devour men.' If the principles of Yang and Mo be not stopped, and the principles of Confucius not set forth, then those perverse speakings will delude the people, and stop up the path of benevolence and righteousness. When benevolence and righteousness are stopped up, beasts will be led on to devour men, and men will devour one another. I am alarmed by these things, and address myself to the defence of the doctrines of the former sages, and to oppose Yang and Mo. I drive away their licentious expressions, so that such perverse speakers may not be able to show themselves. Their delusions spring up in men's minds, and do injury to their practice of affairs. Shown in their practice of affairs, they are pernicious to their government. When sages shall rise up again, they will not change my words.

"In former times, Yu repressed the vast waters of the inundation, and the country was reduced to order. Zhougong's achievements extended even to the barbarous tribes of the east and north, and he drove away all ferocious animals, and the people enjoyed repose. Confucius completed the *Spring and Autumn*, and rebellious ministers and villainous sons were struck with terror. It is said in the *Book of Poetry*, 'He smote the barbarians of the west and the north, he punished Jing and Shu; and no one dared to resist us.' These father deniers and king deniers would have been smitten by Zhougong. I also wish to rectify men's hearts, and to put an end to those perverse doctrines, to oppose their one-sided actions and banish away their licentious expressions; —and thus to carry on the work of the three sages. Do I do so because I am fond of disputing? I am compelled to do it. Whoever is able to oppose Yang and Mo is a disciple of the sages."

【注释】［1］公都子：孟子的弟子。［2］营窟：相连的洞穴。［3］菹（jū）：多水草的沼泽地。［4］作：兴起。［5］飞廉：纣宠爱的臣子。海隅：海滨。［6］恣：放纵。［7］处士：未出仕的士人。横议：胡乱发表言论。［8］闲：本义为栅栏，引申为捍卫。［9］距：通"拒"，排斥。［10］放：贬斥，驳斥。［11］承：抵御。［12］诐（bì）行：不正当的行为。

【译文】公都子说："别人都说您喜好辩论，请问是为什么呢？"

孟子说："我难道喜好辩论吗？我是不得已啊。天下有人类社会很久了，时而太平，时而动乱。在尧的时候，洪水横流，在中原地区泛滥。到处被龙蛇盘踞，民众无处安身。低处的人在树上筑巢，高处的人在山上挖洞。《尚书》说：'洚水告诫了我们。'所谓洚水，就是洪水。于是尧派禹去治理，禹掘地引水注入大海，把龙蛇驱赶到沼泽地。水沿着地上的沟道流动，这就是大江、淮水、黄河、汉水。水患既已解除，鸟兽不再危害人们，百姓们才得以在平原上居住。

"尧、舜去世以后，圣人之道逐渐衰微。暴君接连出现，毁坏了居室来做池沼，使民众无处安身；废弃了农田来做园苑，使民众不能谋生。邪说、暴行随之兴起，园苑、池沼、草泽增多并招来了禽兽。到了商纣时，天下又大乱了。周公辅佐武王诛杀商纣、讨伐奄国，与这些暴君征战了三年，把飞廉赶到海边处死。灭掉的国家有五十个，将虎、豹、犀、象驱赶得远远的，天下的民众都非常喜悦。《尚书》说：'多么英明伟大啊，文王的谋略！继承发扬光大啊，武王的功业！帮助开导我们后人，都走正道而没丝毫缺陷。'

"周室衰微，正道荒废，邪说、暴行随之兴起，臣属杀害自己君主的事出现了，儿子杀害自己父亲的事出现了。孔子为之忧虑，写了《春秋》。《春秋》所记述的是天子的事，因此孔子说：'使世人了解我的恐怕只有《春秋》了，使世人责怪我的恐怕只有《春秋》了。'

"圣王不出现，诸侯肆无忌惮，在野人士横加议论，杨朱、墨翟的言论充斥天下。世上的言论，不属于杨朱一派便属于墨翟一派。杨家主张为我，是不要君王；墨家主张兼爱，是不要父母。不要父母、不要君王就是禽兽。公明仪说：'厨房里有肥肉，马厩里有肥马，而民众却脸带饥色，野外有饿死的人，这是放任野兽去吃人。'杨墨的学说不破除，孔子的学说不发扬，就是用邪说来欺骗民众，遏止仁义的施行。仁义被遏止就是放任野兽去吃人，人们将会相互残杀。我为此感到忧虑，所以捍卫先圣的学说，抵制杨墨的学说，批驳错误的言论，使邪说歪理不再流行。邪说兴起在人们的心中，会危害他们所做的事情；事情受到危害，也就会危害他所施行的政务。即使圣人再度兴起，也不会改变我的结论。

"过去禹制服了洪水使天下太平，周公兼并夷狄、驱赶猛兽使百姓安定，孔子写成《春秋》使作乱的臣属、不孝的儿子害怕。《诗经》说：'攻击北方的戎狄，惩罚南方的荆、舒，就无人能抵御我。'不要父母、不要君王，是周公所要痛击的。我也想去端正人心，破除邪说，抵制偏颇的行为，批驳错误的言论，来继承三位圣人事业。我难道喜好辩论吗？我是不得已啊！敢于抵制杨墨学说的人，就是圣人的门徒。"

【解读】孟子好辩，事关天道人伦、君臣大义，事关公道人心、民生福祉，能不辩乎？孟子之辩，是本着士的良心，带着以天下为己任的责任感而辩，大有"为天地立心，为生民立命，为往圣继绝学，为万世开太平"（张载《横渠语录》）之气概。孟子所处的时代，单从思想层面而言，可谓是百花齐放、百家争鸣，其中不乏与儒家思想相抵触者。从"杨朱、墨翟之言盈天下。天下之言，不归杨，则归墨"一语可以看出，彼时的儒家学说面临极大挑战。天降大任，孟子以"舍我其谁"的担当，来捍卫并复兴孔子之道。杨朱提倡"贵己""为我""轻物重生"，墨子讲"兼相爱，交相利"，这两种极端从根本上是与孔子的中庸之道相悖的，是与仁爱精神背道而驰的。因为"邪说诬民，充塞仁义"，所以，孟子要辩，也不能不辩。唯有辩，方能去歪理，止邪说；

唯有辩，方能正人心，明四端（恻隐、羞恶、辞让、是非）；唯有辩，方能拨乱象，成大治。尽管在天下大乱、王纲解纽、礼崩乐坏的战国时代，孟子之辩有些不合时宜，但置于人类历史的长河中，我们就会发现，孟子之辩，既有其时代的必要性，更有其超出时代的前瞻性。其仁政主张，其民本思想，至今仍熠熠生辉。

6.10

匡章[1]曰："陈仲子[2]岂不诚廉士哉？居於陵[3]，三日不食，耳无闻，目无见也。井上有李，螬[4]食实者过半矣，匍匐往将[5]食之，三咽，然后耳有闻，目有见。"

孟子曰："于齐国之士，吾必以仲子为巨擘[6]焉。虽然，仲子恶能廉？充仲子之操，则蚓而后可者也。夫蚓，上食槁壤，下饮黄泉。仲子所居之室，伯夷之所筑与？抑亦盗跖[7]之所筑与？所食之粟，伯夷之所树与？抑亦盗跖之所树与？是未可知也。"

曰："是何伤哉？彼身织屦，妻辟纑[8]，以易之也。"

曰："仲子，齐之世家也。兄戴，盖禄万钟[9]。以兄之禄为不义之禄而不食也，以兄之室为不义之室而不居也，辟兄离母，处于於陵。他日归，则有馈其兄生鹅者，己频顑[10]曰：'恶用是鶃鶃[11]者为哉？'他日，其母

杀是鹅也，与之食之。其兄自外至，曰：'是
鶃鶃之肉也。'出而哇^[12]之。以母则不食，
以妻则食之；以兄之室则弗居，以於陵则居之。
是尚为能充其类也乎？若仲子者，蚓而后充
其操者也。"

Kuang Zhang said to Mencius, "Is not Chen
Zhong a man of true self-denying purity? He was
living in Wuling, and for three days was without
food, till he could neither hear nor see. Over a
well there grew a plum tree, the fruit of which had
been more than half eaten by worms. He crawled
to it, and tried to eat some of the fruit, when, after
swallowing three mouthfuls, he recovered his sight
and hearing. "

Mencius replied, "Among the scholars of Qi, I
must regard Zhong as the thumb among the fingers.
But still, where is the self-denying purity he pretends
to? To carry out the principles which he holds, one

must become an earthworm, for so only can it be done. Now, an earthworm eats the dry mould above, and drinks the yellow spring below. Was the house in which Zhong dwells built by a Boyi? or was it built by a robber like Zhi? Was the millet which he eats planted by a Boyi? Or was it planted by a robber like Zhi? These are things which cannot be known."

"But," said Zhang, "what does that matter? He himself weaves sandals of hemp, and his wife twists and dresses threads of hemp to sell or exchange them."

Mencius rejoined, "Zhong belongs to an ancient and noble family of Qi. His elder brother Dai received from Gai a revenue of 10,000 *zhong*, but he considered his brother's emolument to be unrighteous, and would not eat of it, and in the same way he considered his brother's house to be unrighteous, and would not dwell in it. Avoiding his brother and leaving his mother, he went and dwelt in Wuling. One day afterwards, he returned to their house, when it happened that some one sent his brother a present of a live goose. He, knitting his eyebrows, said, 'What are you going to use that cackling thing for?' By-and-by his mother killed the goose, and gave him some of it to eat. Just then his brother came into the house, and said, 'It is the flesh of that cackling thing,' upon which he went out and vomited it. Thus, what his mother gave him he would not eat, but what his wife gives him he eats. He will not dwell in his brother's house, but he dwells in Wuling. How can he in such circumstances complete the style of life which he professes? With such principles as Zhong holds, a man must be an earthworm, and then he can carry them out."

【注释】［１］匡章：齐国名将，为孟子友人。［２］陈仲子：齐国人，因居住在於（wū）陵，后人称他为於陵子。［3］於陵：齐国地名，有学者考证其故址位于今邹平市临池镇古城村。［4］蟮（cáo）：金龟子的幼虫。［5］将：拿、取。［6］巨擘（bò）：大拇指，引申为在某一方面了不起的人物。［7］盗跖（zhí）：春秋时有名的大盗，传说为柳下惠的兄弟。［8］辟纑（lú）：绩麻练麻。辟，绩麻。纑，练麻。［9］盖（gě）：地名，是陈戴的封邑。钟：古代计量单位，春秋时齐国以十釜为"钟"，这里可理解为"厚禄"。［10］频顣（cù）：即"颦蹙"，愁眉苦脸不愉快的样子。［11］鶂鶂（yì）：鹅的叫声。［12］哇：吐。

【译文】匡章说："陈仲子难道不是一个真正廉洁的人吗？住在於陵这个地方，三天没有吃东西，耳朵听不见，眼睛看不见。井上有个李子，金龟子的幼虫已经吃掉了一大半，他爬过去拿过来吃，吞了三口，耳朵才听得见了，眼睛才看得见了。"

孟子说："在齐国士人中间，我一定把仲子看作了不起的人物。但是，他怎么能算作廉洁？要推广仲子的操守，那只有把人变成蚯蚓之后才能办到。蚯蚓，在地面上吃干土，在地面下喝泉水。可仲子所住的房屋，是像伯夷那样廉洁的人所建筑的呢，还是像盗跖那样的强盗所建筑的呢？他所吃的粮食，是像伯夷那样廉洁的人所种植的呢，还是像盗跖那样的强盗所种植的呢？这个还是不知道的。"

匡章说："那有什么妨碍呢？他亲自编草鞋，妻子绩麻练麻，用这些去交换来的。"

孟子说："仲子生在齐国的宗族世家，他的哥哥陈戴在盖邑的俸禄有万钟之多。可他却认为他哥哥的俸禄是不义之财而不去吃，认为他哥哥的住房是不义之产而不去住，避开哥哥，离开母亲，住在於陵。有一天他回家里，正好看到有人送给他哥哥一只鹅，他皱着眉头说：'要这种呃呃叫的东西做什么呢？'过了几天，他母亲把鹅杀了给他吃。他的哥哥恰好从外面回来，看见后便说：'你吃的正是那呃呃叫的东西的肉啊！'他连忙跑出门去，'哇'的一声便呕吐了出来。母亲的食物不吃，却吃妻子的；哥哥的房屋不住，却住在於陵，他所推崇的行为能够体现在其一贯的行为中吗？像他那样做，只有把人变成蚯蚓之后才能够办到。"

【解读】此章写匡章问"廉"，陈仲子异于常人的行为难道不是真正的廉洁之士吗？但在孟子看来，陈仲子之"廉"难以令人信服，所以孟子回答说，像陈仲子这样的"廉"只有变成蚯蚓才能完全做到，这就直接否定了陈仲子之廉。那么，为什么孟子会如此评价陈仲子呢？

首先，陈仲子之廉具有客观上的不可操作性和无法示范性。廉，并非不食人间烟火，陈仲子"三日不食，耳无闻，目无见"，命都难保了，如此之廉又有何用？如果人人学习陈仲子，那偌大天下岂不变成了一个自虐的国度？

其次，陈仲子之廉还具有客观上的违背人伦和不合道义性。仲子为廉别母另居，是为不孝；为廉诋毁兄长，是为不悌。孝悌大义都抛之脑后了，廉又有什么意义？为廉而别居，实则是对现实的畏惧和逃避，实则是不讲责任、不敢担当的懦夫行为。

第三，陈仲子之廉具有主观上的荒谬性和欺骗性。"以母则不食，以妻则食之"，兄长的房子不住，而去不知何人修建的房子里住，可谓荒谬至极，让人无法不怀疑其动机。究其实质也不过是欺世盗名罢了。

因此，陈仲子之廉不过是徒有其名的假廉义、伪道学罢了。真正的廉，应该是廉而有义、廉而有节、廉而有度。伯夷、叔齐为义不食周粟饿死首阳山是为廉，其廉在于忠臣不事二主；颜回一箪食、一瓢饮是为廉，其廉在于安贫乐道。当今社会，孔繁森扎根雪域高原是为廉，其廉在于对党的忠诚和对人民的奉献。廉，只能由百姓心中的标尺来测量。

离娄上

Li Lou 1

7.1

孟子曰："离娄[1]之明，公输子[2]之巧，不以规矩，不能成方员[3]；师旷[4]之聪，不以六律[5]，不能正五音[6]；尧、舜之道，不以仁政，不能平治天下。今有仁心仁闻[7]而民不被其泽，不可法于后世者，不行先王之道也。故曰，徒善不足以为政，徒法不能以自行。《诗》云：'不愆不忘，率由旧章[8]。'遵先王之法而过者，未之有也。圣人既竭目力焉，继之以规矩准绳，以为方员平直，不可胜用也；既竭耳力焉，继之以六律，正五音，不可胜用也；既竭心思焉，继之以不忍人之政，而仁覆天下矣。故曰，为高必因丘陵，为下必因川泽。为政不因先王之道，可谓智乎？是以惟仁者宜在高位。不仁而在高位，是播其恶于众也。上无道揆[9]也，下无法守也，朝不信道，工不信度，君子犯义，小人犯刑，国之所存者幸也。故曰，城郭不完，兵甲不多，非国之灾也；田野不辟，货财不聚，非国之害也。上无礼，下无学，贼民兴，丧无日矣。《诗》曰：'天之方蹶，无然泄泄[10]。'泄泄，犹沓沓[11]也。事君无义，进退无礼，言则非先王之道者，犹沓沓也。故曰：责难于君谓之恭，陈善闭[12]邪谓之敬，吾君不能谓之贼。"

Mencius said, "The power of vision of Li Lou, and skill of hand of Gongshu, without the compass and square, could not form squares and circles. The acute ear of the music-master Kuang, without the pitch-tubes, could not determine correctly the five notes. The principles of Yao and Shun, without a benevolent government, could not secure the tranquil order of the kingdom. There are now princes who have benevolent hearts and a reputation for benevolence, while yet the people do not receive any benefits from them, nor will they leave any example to future ages; —all because they do not put into practice the ways of the ancient kings. Hence we have the saying: 'Virtue alone is not sufficient for the exercise of government; laws alone cannot carry themselves into practice.' It is said in the *Book of Poetry*, 'Without transgression, without forgetfulness, following the ancient statutes.' Never has any one fallen into error, who followed the laws of the ancient kings. When the sages had used the vigour of their eyes, they called in to their aid the compass, the square, the level, and the line, to make things square, round, level, and straight: —the use of the instruments is inexhaustible. When they had used their power of hearing to the utmost, they called in the pitch-tubes to their aid to determine the five notes: —the use of those tubes is inexhaustible. When they had exerted to the utmost the thoughts of their hearts, they called in to their aid a government that could not endure to witness the sufferings of men —and their benevolence overspread the kingdom. Hence we have the saying: 'To raise a thing high, we must begin from the top of a mound or a hill; to dig to a great depth, we must commence in the low ground of a stream or a marsh.' Can he be pronounced wise, who, in the exercise of government, does not proceed according to the ways of the former kings? Therefore only the benevolent ought to be in high stations. When a man destitute of benevolence is in a high station, he thereby disseminates his wickedness among all below him. When the prince has no principles by which he examines his administration, and his ministers have no laws by which they keep themselves in the discharge of their duties, then in the court obedience is not paid to principle, and in the office obedience is not paid to rule. Superiors violate the laws of righteousness, and inferiors violate the penal laws. It is only by a fortunate chance that a state in such a case is preserved. Therefore it is said, 'It is not the exterior and interior walls being incomplete, and the supply of weapons offensive and defensive not being large, which constitutes the calamity of a kingdom. It is not the cultivable area not being extended, and stores and wealth not being accumulated, which occasions the ruin of a state.' When superiors do not observe the rules of propriety, and inferiors do not learn, then seditious people spring up, and that state will perish in no time. It is said in the *Book of Poetry*, 'When such an overthrow of Zhou is being produced by Heaven, be not ye so much at your ease!' 'At your ease;' —that is, dilatory. And so dilatory may those officers be deemed, who serve their prince without righteousness, who take office and retire from it without regard to propriety, and who in their words disown the ways of the ancient kings. Therefore it is said, 'To urge one's sovereign to difficult achievements may be called showing respect for him. To set before him what is good and repress

his perversities may be called showing reverence
for him. He who does not do these things, saying to
himself, 'My sovereign is incompetent to this, may
be said to play the thief with him.'"

【注释】[1]离娄：相传为黄帝时人，目力极强，
可以在百步之外望见秋毫之末。[2]公输子：
即鲁班，春秋末年的能工巧匠。[3]方员：
同"方圆"。[4]师旷：春秋时晋国的乐师。[5]
六律：古代乐音标准名。乐律有十二，阴阳
各六，阳为律，阴为吕。六律即黄钟、太簇、
姑洗、蕤宾、夷则、无射。[6]五音：古代
音阶名称，即宫、商、角、徵、羽，相当于
简谱中的1、2、3、5、6五音。[7]闻：声
誉，名声。[8]不愆（qiān）不忘，率由旧章：
引自《诗经·大雅·假乐》。愆，过失。率，
遵循。[9]揆（kuí）：度量。[10]天之方蹶，
无然泄（yì）泄：引自《诗经·大雅·板》。蹶：
动，颠覆。泄泄：多言，话多。[11]沓沓：

语多。〔12〕闭：排斥。

【译文】孟子说："即使有离娄那样好的视力，公输子那样巧的手艺，如果不用圆规和曲尺，也不能准确地画出方形和圆形；即使有师旷那样好的听力，如果不用六律，也不能校正五音；即使有尧、舜之道，如果不实施仁政，也不能治理好天下。现在有些诸侯，虽然有仁爱的心和仁爱的名声，但老百姓受不到他的恩泽，也不能成为后世效法的楷模，这是因为他没有实施前代圣王的仁政。所以说，只有好心不足以治理好天下，只有法度，也不能够自行实施。《诗经》说：'不犯错误不遗忘，一切遵循过去的规章。'遵循前代圣王的法度而犯错误的，是从来没有过的。圣人既用尽了目力，又用规矩准绳等来制作方、圆、平、直，这些东西都用不完；既用尽了听力，再加上六律，校正五音就绰绰有余；既用尽了心思，再加上施行仁政，仁义便能遍布天下了。所以说，筑高台一定要凭借山陵，凿深池一定要凭借河泽。施政不继承先王之道，能说是明智吗？所以只有仁者适宜在高位。如果不仁爱的人占据了高位，就会把他的恶行传播给老百姓。在上位的人没有道德规范，在下位的人没有法规制度，朝廷不信道义，工匠不信尺度，官吏触犯义理，百姓触犯刑律，如此下去，国家还能存在就真是太侥幸了。所以说，城墙不坚固，武器不充足，这不是国家的灾难；田野没开辟，物资不积聚，也不是国家的祸害。如果在上位的人没有礼义，在下位的人没有学识，违法乱纪的人越来越多，国家的灭亡也就快了。《诗经》说：'上天要颠覆他，就不要多嘴了。'多嘴多言就是啰嗦的意思。侍奉君主不讲忠义，进退失礼，说话便诋毁前代圣王之道，这就是多嘴啰嗦。所以说，用高标准来要求君王就叫作'恭'，向君王宣讲善义摈弃邪说就叫作'敬'，认为君王不能行仁政就叫作'贼'。"

《孟子》插图

孟子曰：离娄之明，公输子之巧，不以规矩，不能
成方圆；师旷之聪，不以六律，不能正五音；尧舜之道，
不以仁政，不能平治天下。今有仁心仁闻而民不被其泽，不可
法于后世者，不行先王之道也。岁次庚子之春 永生画之

不以仁政，不能平治天下　徐永生 绘

【解读】治政之要，首先在于仁者仁心。孟子认为"先王有不忍人之心，斯有不忍人之政矣"（《孟子·公孙丑上》），把一个国家治理好，首先就要求这个国家的君主是一个仁者，有仁爱之心，这是施行仁政的先决条件。

孟子还认为，治理国家、施行仁政只有仁心是远远不够的，还必须有善法。国有善法，就好比画方圆之有规矩，正五音之有六律一样。国无善法，"上无道揆也，下无法守也"，就会导致"朝不信道，工不信度，君子犯义，小人犯刑"的混乱局面，就会"上无礼，下无学，贼民兴，丧无日矣"，此乃国之灾、国之害的要点。具体来看，孟子所强调的法就是法先王，效法尧舜那样的圣君行仁义，施仁政。于君而言，不仅要有仁心，也不能仅仅以仁为口号，更要效法尧舜将仁具体化为一项项的仁政措施。于臣而言，要以礼侍君，要以义侍君，核心就是劝谏君主效法先王讲仁义、行仁政，这才是对君主真正的恭和敬。否则，便是贼君害民。要之，无论何时，仁都是判断良政的标尺。我们今天讲依法治国、依法行政，讲立德树人、以德治国，更应高扬"仁"这面大旗。

7.2

孟子曰："规矩，方员之至也；圣人，人伦之至也。欲为君尽君道；欲为臣尽臣道，二者皆法尧、舜而已矣。不以舜之所以事尧事君，不敬其君者也；不以尧之所以治民治民，贼其民者也。孔子曰：'道二：仁与不仁而已矣。'暴其民甚，则身弑国亡；不甚，则身危国削。名之曰'幽厉'[1]，虽孝子慈孙，百世不能改也。《诗》云'殷鉴不远，在夏后之世'[2]，此之谓也。"

Mencius said, "The compass and square produce perfect circles and squares. By the sages, the human relations are perfectly exhibited. He who as a sovereign would perfectly discharge the duties of a sovereign, and he who as a minister would perfectly discharge the duties of a minister, have only to imitate—the one Yao, and the other Shun.

He who does not serve his sovereign as Shun served Yao, does not respect his sovereign; and he who does not rule his people as Yao ruled his, injures his people. Confucius said, 'There are but two courses, which can be pursued, that of virtue and its opposite.' A ruler who carries the oppression of his people to the highest pitch, will himself be slain, and his kingdom will perish. If one stop short of the highest pitch, his life will notwithstanding be in danger, and his kingdom will be weakened. He will be styled 'The Dark' or 'The Cruel,' and though he may have filial sons and affectionate grandsons, they will not be able in a hundred generations to change the designation. This is what is intended in the words of the *Book of Poetry*, 'The beacon of Yin is not remote, it is in the time of the sovereign of Xia.' "

【注释】［1］幽：昏暗。厉：暴虐。在古代的谥号中，皆属恶谥。周幽王沉湎于酒色，信

用佞臣，甚昏昧，故谥"幽"。周厉王暴虐，
故谥"厉"。［2］殷鉴不远，在夏后之世：
引自《诗经·大雅·荡》。鉴：镜，指借鉴。

【译文】孟子说："规和矩，是方形和圆形的
最高标准；圣人，是做人的最高标准。想做
国君就应尽国君之道，想做臣属就应尽臣属
之道，这两者都是效法尧舜而已。不以舜服
事尧那样来服事君主，就是不敬自己的君主；
不以尧治理民众那样来治理民众，就是残害
自己的民众。孔子说：'道有两种：仁与不
仁罢了。'暴虐民众过分了，就会身死国丧；
即便不太过分，也会自身危险、国力削弱，
赐谥号为'幽''厉'，即使有孝子慈孙，
经百世之后这名声也不能改变。《诗经》说：
'殷商的借鉴并不遥远，就在它的前代夏朝。'
就是这个意思。"

【解读】儒家强调伦理道德，指向有二：一为血

缘伦理，用以调和父子、夫妻关系；一为政治伦理，用以调和君臣关系。君臣之伦，是人之大伦，儒家要实现治国平天下的梦想，必须妥善处理君与臣的关系。孟子论述君臣关系，一方面提出了君臣关系的榜样与典型：做君，就做尧那样的君；做臣，就做舜那样的臣。另一方面，孟子又强调了一个"道"字：为君，就要尽君道；为臣，就要尽臣道，道的核心就是"仁"。"仁"不仅成为衡量君、臣是否称职的一把标尺，更是调和君臣关系的不二法门。不合仁道之君，谓之独夫，被民众怨恨而诛之，被谥为"幽""厉"，遗臭万年；不合仁道之臣，谓之贼，贼君害民之人，也会永远被钉在历史的耻辱柱上。君臣都能本于仁，据于礼，行于义，才能上下和睦，政通人和。于今而言，人人各安其位，各守其道，以仁的高标准要求自己，方能实现人际关系的和谐，从而促进整个社会的安定与和谐。

7.3

孟子曰："三代^[1]之得天下也以仁，其失天下也以不仁。国之所以废兴存亡者亦然。天子不仁，不保四海；诸侯不仁，不保社稷；卿大夫不仁，不保宗庙^[2]；士庶人不仁，不保四体。今恶死亡而乐不仁，是犹恶醉而强^[3]酒。"

Mencius said, "It was by benevolence that the three dynasties gained the throne, and by not being benevolent that they lost it. It is by the same means that the decaying and flourishing, the preservation and perishing of states, are determined. If the sovereign be not benevolent, he cannot preserve the throne from passing from him. If the Head of a State be not benevolent, he cannot preserve his rule. If a high noble or great officer be not benevolent, he cannot preserve his ancestral temple. If a scholar or common man be not benevolent, be cannot preserve his four limbs. Now they hate death and ruin, and yet delight in being not benevolent—this is like hating to be drunk, and yet being strong to drink wine!"

【注释】 [1]三代：指夏、商、周。[2]宗庙：天子、诸侯祭祀祖先的庙堂。[3]强：勉强。

【译文】 孟子说："夏、商、周三个朝代得到了天下是由于仁，失去天下是由于不仁。诸侯国的兴衰存亡也是因为同样的原因。天子不仁爱，天下就不保；诸侯不仁爱，国家就不保；卿大夫不仁爱，祖庙就不保；士人和平民百姓不仁爱，自身就不保。如今的人害怕死亡而又以行不仁之事为乐，这就如同害怕醉酒却偏要勉强多喝酒一样。"

【解读】 汤、武之兴，在于行仁；桀、纣之亡，

在于不仁。在孟子看来，仁是人间一种衡量
废兴存亡的标尺。无论天子、诸侯、卿大夫
还是士、庶人，只有行仁，方能保天下、保
国家、保宗庙、保自身。仁者兴，不仁者亡，
这是不可抗拒的历史规律。既想要国家兴盛，
称王于诸侯，又暴虐其民不施仁政，这种行
为无异于厌恶喝醉却要强行喝酒，无异于饮
鸩止渴。对于今天的领导干部来说，讲求仁，
施行仁，就是要多行惠民、利民之实，不做
扰民、害民之事。

7.4

孟子曰："爱人不亲反[1]其仁，治人不治反其智[2]，礼人不答反其敬。行有不得者，皆反求诸己，其身正而天下归之。《诗》云：'永言配命，自求多福[3]。'"

Mencius said, "If a man love others, and no responsive attachment is shown to him, let him turn inwards and examine his own benevolence. If he is trying to rule others, and his government is unsuccessful, let him turn inwards and examine his wisdom. If he treats others politely, and they do not return his politeness, let him turn inwards and examine his own feeling of respect. When we do not, by what we do, realise what we desire, we must turn inwards, and examine ourselves in every point. When a man's person is correct, the whole kingdom will turn to him with recognition and submission. It is said in the *Book of Poetry*, 'Be always studious to be in harmony with the ordinances of God, and you will obtain much happiness.' "

【注释】［1］反：反省。［2］智：才智。［3］永言配命，自求多福：出自《诗经·大雅·文王》。言：语助词。配命：配合天命。

【译文】孟子说："爱别人而没有得到别人的亲近，那就要反思自己的仁爱是否有问题；管理百姓而没有管理好，那就要反思自己的智慧能力是否有问题；礼貌待人而别人不理会，那就应反思自己的礼敬是否有问题。所作所为得不到预期效果，都应该从自身找原因，自身行为端正，天下的人就会归服。《诗经》有言：'永远要配合天命，自己努力才会多福。'"

【解读】"反求诸己"是儒家为人处世的态度，

也是一种重要的思维方式和方法。孔子说："君子求诸己，小人求诸人。"（《论语·卫灵公》）当我们在学习、生活中遇到种种矛盾、种种问题时，首先应进行自我反省，从自身寻找原因，这不仅是个人修养的一种体现，也是和谐人际关系的一种需要，更是问题顺利解决的不二法门。很多时候，矛盾和问题之所以存在，就是因为我们忽视了"反求诸己"，忽视了推己及人。熊十力先生曾说："先圣贤之学，广大悉备，而一点血脉，只是'反求诸己'四字。"（《十力语要》）可以这样说，圣贤之所以为圣贤，就在于其有常人所不具备的"反求诸己"的品质，就在于他们能够躬亲自省，严以律己。

其身正而天下歸之

语出孟子离娄句 仲亭

录《孟子》句 张仲亭 书

7.5

孟子曰："人有恒[1]言，皆曰'天下国家'。天下之本在国，国之本在家，家之本在身。"

Mencius said, "People have this common saying, 'The kingdom, the state, the family.' The root of the kingdom is in the state. The root of the state is in the family. The root of the family is in the person of its head.' "

【注释】［1］恒：常。

【译文】孟子说："人们常说一句话，都说'天下国家'。天下的基础在国，国的基础在家，家的基础在自身。"

【解读】"天下国家"，是人们常常说起的，但是，很多人不知其间的关系。朱熹《四书章句集注》曰："虽常言之，而未必知其言之有序也。故推言之，而又以家本乎身也。此亦承上章而言之。《大学》所谓'自天子至于庶人，壹是皆以修身为本'。"孟子认为，天下的基础是国，国的基础是家，家的基础是家庭中的每一个人。因此，人是最根本的。所以《大学》中如此说："古之欲明明德于天下者，先治其国；欲治其国者，先齐其家；欲齐其家者，先修其身……身修而后家齐，家齐而后国治，国治而后天下平。"孟子此说的用意是，不要只是口头上念叨"天下国家"，而是要明白"天下国家"的次序关系，明白自身的修为和担当。一个真正具有家国情怀的人，要自觉地从根本（自身）做起，做"修身、齐家、治国、平天下"的真正践行者。

天下国家　卢冰　绘

7.6

孟子曰："为政不难，不得罪于巨室^[1]。巨室之所慕，一国慕之；一国之所慕，天下慕之，故沛然德教溢乎四海。"

Mencius said, "The administration of government is not difficult; —it lies in not offending the great families. He whom the great families affect, will be affected by the whole state, and he whom any one state affects, will be affected by the whole kingdom. When this is the case, such an one's virtue and teachings will spread over all within the four seas like the rush of water."

【注释】［1］巨室：世家大族。赵岐注曰："巨室，大家也，谓贤卿大夫之家。"

【译文】孟子说："从事政治并不难，只要不得罪那些贤明的望族世家。因为他们所思慕的，一国人都会思慕；一国人思慕的，天下人都会思慕。因此，道德的教化就会浩浩荡荡地流布天下。"

【解读】本章接上章之"仁"而谈，孟子告诫治国理政者，要倚重贤明的世家大族。首先，这些世家大族是当世成功者，具有丰富的治家理政的成功经验。再者，由于他们贤明，有地位，有声望，因而具有强大的影响力和号召力。一般情况下，这部分人所想的，正是国民想要的。借重这些世家大族的威望和影响力，尊重他们先进的理政思路，那么天下就会出现仁德教化充溢、政通人和的美好局面。

7.7

孟子曰："天下有道，小德役[1]大德，小贤役大贤；天下无道，小役大，弱役强。斯二者天也。顺天者存，逆天者亡。齐景公曰：'既不能令，又不受命，是绝物[2]也。'涕出而女于吴[3]。今也小国师大国而耻受命焉，是犹弟子而耻受命于先师也。如耻之，莫若师文王。师文王，大国五年，小国七年，必为政于天下矣。《诗》云：'商之孙子，其丽不亿[4]。上帝既命，侯于周服。侯服[5]于周，天命靡常。殷士肤敏[6]，祼将于京[7]。'孔子曰：'仁不可为众也。夫国君好仁，天下无敌。'今也欲无敌于天下而不以仁，是犹执热而不以濯也[8]。《诗》云：'谁能执热，逝不以濯[9]？'"

Mencius said, "When right government prevails in the kingdom, princes of little virtue are submissive to those of great, and those of little worth to those of great. When bad government prevails in the kingdom, princes of small power are submissive to those of great, and the weak to the strong. Both these cases are the rule of Heaven. They who accord with Heaven are preserved, and they who rebel against Heaven perish. The duke Jing of Qi said, 'Not to be able to command others, and at the same time to refuse to receive their commands, is to cut one's self off from all intercourse with others.' His tears flowed forth while he gave his daughter to be married to the prince of Wu. Now the small states imitate the large, and yet are ashamed to receive their commands. This is like a scholar's being ashamed to receive the commands of his master. For a prince who is ashamed of this, the best plan is to imitate king Wen. Let one imitate king Wen, and in five years, if his state be large, or in seven years, if it be small, he will be sure to give laws to the kingdom. It is said in the *Book of Poetry*, 'The descendants of the sovereigns of the Shang dynasty, are in number more than hundreds of thousands; but, God having passed His decree, they are all submissive to Zhou. They are submissive to Zhou, because the decree of Heaven is not unchanging. The officers of Yin, admirable and alert, pour out the libations, and assist in the capital of Zhou.' Confucius said, 'As against so benevolent a sovereign, they could not be deemed a multitude.' Thus, if the prince of a state love benevolence, he will have no opponent in all the kingdom. Now they wish to have no opponent in all the kingdom, but they do not seek to attain this by being benevolent. This is like a man laying hold of a heated substance, and not having first dipped it in water. It is said in the *Book of Poetry*, 'Who can take up a heated substance, without first dipping it(in water)?' "

【注释】［1］役：役使，听命。［2］绝物：

断绝人事交往。［3］女于吴：把女儿嫁到吴国和亲，以求出路。［4］丽：数目。不亿：不下亿万。［5］侯服：古代王域外围。夏制称离王域一千里的地方，周制称王域周围方千里以外的方五百里的地区。郑玄《周礼注》曰："服，服事天子也。"［6］肤敏：优美敏捷。［7］裸（guàn）：古代祭祀的仪式，把酒洒在地上迎神。将：助祭。此诗句出自《诗经·大雅·文王》。［8］执热：手持灼热之物。濯：洗。［9］谁能执热，逝不以濯：朱熹《四书章句集注》曰："言谁能执持热物，而不以水自濯其手乎？"此诗句见于《诗经·大雅·桑柔》。

【译文】孟子说："如果天下有道，道德不高的人听命于道德高的人，小贤之人听命于大贤之人；如果天下无道，力量小的就会被力量大的所役使，势弱的就会被势强的所役使。这两种情况都是天命所决定的。顺从天命则

生存，违背天命则灭亡。齐景公说：'既不
能号令他人，又不愿服从命令，这是自绝于
世。'景公因此流着眼泪把女儿嫁到了吴国。
现在小国以大国为师却又以受命于大国为耻，
这如同学生耻于听从师命一样。如果以此为
耻，不如师从周文王。师从周文王，大国只
需五年，小国只需七年，一定会统治整个天下。
《诗经》有言：'殷商的子孙后代，其数不
下亿万。上帝既已授命于周，就应臣服于周。
臣服于周，说明天命无常。殷朝的臣子虽然
漂亮聪敏，如今也只得在周王京城洒酒助祭。'
孔子说：'仁的力量不是以人数多少来衡量的。
国君爱好仁德，就能天下无敌。' 如今想要
无敌于天下，却不施行仁政，如同手持灼热
之物而不用凉水冲洗一样。《诗经》说：'谁
能手持灼热之物，却不用凉水冲洗？'"

【解读】孟子之谓天，是指天人合一之天，是一
种人不可违背的自然规律。孟子说："尽其心

者，知其性也；知其性，则知天矣。"（《孟子·尽心上》）人若能够尽心知性，有足够的修养，便能知天道，达到天人合一的境界。其核心在于仁，当人人崇尚德行，有仁德者居于主导地位时，就会社会安定，秩序井然，人民安居乐业，是为有道之天，如尧舜时代。当社会崇尚武力，不仁者居于主导地位时，就会社会动荡，战乱频仍，人民颠沛流离，这是无道之天，如孟子所处的战国时代。把社会的治乱归结于天意，说"顺天者存，逆天者亡"，具有一定的唯心主义色彩，这是孟子的局限所在。但孟子又强调人对于天的主观能动性，强调仁者无敌，可谓真知灼见。人在天面前特别是在"无道之天"面前不是任其宰割、无所作为的，而是通过加强个人修养，讲仁德、行仁政的方式变无道为有道，从而无敌于天下。这不啻为改变无道之天的必由之途，给乱世开出的疗疾良方。无论过去还是现在，孟子的仁政思想都闪烁着不可磨灭的光辉。

7.8

孟子曰："不仁者可与言哉？安其危而利其菑 [1]，乐 [2] 其所以亡者。不仁而可与言，则何亡国败家之有？有孺子歌 [3] 曰：'沧浪 [4] 之水清兮，可以濯我缨 [5]；沧浪之水浊兮，可以濯我足。'孔子曰：'小子听之！清斯濯缨，浊斯濯足矣，自取之也。'夫人必自侮，然后人侮之；家必自毁，而后人毁之；国必自伐，而后人伐之。《太甲》曰：'天作孽，犹可违；自作孽，不可活。'此之谓也。"

Mencius said, "How is it possible to speak with those princes who are not benevolent? Their perils they count safety, their calamities they count profitable, and they have pleasure in the things by which they perish. If it were possible to talk with them who so violate benevolence, how could we have such destruction of states and ruin of families?

There was a boy singing, 'When the water of the Canglang is clear, it does to wash the strings of my cap; When the water of the Canglang is muddy, it does to wash my feet.' Confucius said, 'Hear what he sings, my children. When clear, then he will wash his cap-strings; and when muddy, he will wash his feet with it. This different application is brought by the water on itself.' A man must first despise himself, and then others will despise him. A family must first destroy itself, and then others will destroy it. A state must first smite itself, and then others will smite it. This is illustrated in the passage of the *Tai Jia*, 'When Heaven sends down calamities, it is still possible to escape them. When we occasion the calamities ourselves, it is not possible any longer to live.' "

【注释】［1］菑：同"灾"，灾难。［2］乐：沉迷。［3］孺子歌：当时流传很广的民歌。［4］沧浪：前人有多种解释，或认为是水名（汉水支流），或认为是地名（湖北均县镇北），或认为是水的颜色（青苍色）。［5］缨：系帽子的丝带。

【译文】孟子说："不仁的人可以与他交谈吗？他们苟安于危险之中，在灾难中捞取利益，沉迷于让他们丧生的事情当中。如果不仁的人也可以与他讲道理，那怎么会有亡国败家的事呢？小孩子的歌唱道：'沧浪的水清澈啊，可以洗我的冠缨；沧浪的水浑浊啊，可以洗我的脚。'孔子说：'后生们听着！水清则洗冠缨，水浊则洗双脚。这是水决定的。'人必定是自己不尊重自己，别人才会来侮辱；家必定是自毁了，别人才会来毁坏它；国必定是自相攻伐了，别国才会来攻伐它。《太甲》说：'上天降灾还可躲开，自己作孽则无法逃避。'就是这个意思。"

【解读】本章的主旨意在表明：人之安危，取决于自己。以不仁之人的思维方式来思考问题，来为人做事，必定会招致杀身败家误国的灾难。如果能与他们交谈，晓之以理，就不会出现败家亡国之事了。孟子意在强调：凡是亡国败家者，都是自身的原因造成的，即"夫人必自侮，然后人侮之；家必自毁，而后人毁之；国必自伐，而后人伐之"。这一论断给人们带来巨大的教育作用。"安其危而利其菑"的不仁之人古已有之，远的不说，和孟子处于同一时代的张仪、苏秦就是这种人。他们唯恐天下不乱，因为只有"乱"，他们方能坐收渔翁之利，方能"英雄"有用武之地。生灵涂炭、饿殍遍野是不在他们考虑之列的，他们考虑的只是实现个人的抱负、个人的价值。同时，孟子还引用民谣"沧浪之水清兮，可以濯我缨；沧浪之水浊兮，可以濯我足"来寓意抉择仁与不仁。最后，他警告那些统治者，不行仁政就会像《太甲》所说"自作孽，不可活"。在今天看来，战国时代群雄并起、诸侯争霸的最后结局不幸被孟子言中。正如明代张居正所说："有国家者，仁则荣，不仁则辱，祸福皆自己求之，亦岂人之所能与哉？"（《四书集注阐微直解》）无论个人还是国家，都要注重自身，如果不自侮、不自毁、不自伐，别人就很难侮之、毁之、伐之。圣哲给世人敲响的警钟振聋发聩："自作孽，不可活。"好自为之！

7.9

孟子曰："桀、纣之失天下也，失其民也；失其民者，失其心也。得天下有道：得其民，斯得天下矣；得其民有道：得其心，斯得民矣；得其心有道：所欲与之聚之，所恶勿施尔也[1]。民之归仁也，犹水之就下、兽之走圹[2]也。故为渊驱鱼者，獭也；为丛驱爵[3]者，鹯[4]也；为汤武驱民者，桀与纣也。今天下之君有好仁者，则诸侯皆为之驱矣。虽欲无王，不可得已。今之欲王者，犹七年之病求三年之艾[5]也。苟为不畜，终身不得。苟不志于仁，终身忧辱，以陷于死亡。《诗》云'其何能淑，载胥及溺'[6]，此之谓也。"

Mencius said, "Jie and Zhou's losing the throne, arose from their losing the people, and to lose the people means to lose their hearts. There is a way to get the kingdom: —get the people, and the

kingdom is got. There is a way to get the people: —
get their hearts, and the people are got. There is a
way to get their hearts: — it is simply to collect for
them what they like, and not to lay on them what
they dislike. The people turn to a benevolent rule as
water flows downwards, and as wild beasts fly to the
wilderness. Accordingly, as the otter aids the deep
waters, driving the fish into them, and the hawk aids
the thickets, driving the little birds to them, so Jie
and Zhou aided Tang and Wu, driving the people to
them. If among the present rulers of the kingdom,
there were one who loved benevolence, all the other
princes would aid him, by driving the people to him.
Although he wished not to become sovereign, be
could not avoid becoming so. The case of one of the
present princes wishing to become sovereign is like
the having to seek for mugwort three years old, to
cure a seven years' sickness. If it have not been kept
in store, the patient may all his life not get it. If the

princes do not set their wills on benevolence, all their days will be in sorrow and disgrace, and they will be involved in death and ruin. This is illustrated by what is said in the *Book of Poetry*, 'How otherwise can you improve the kingdom? You will only with it go to ruin.' "

【注释】［1］尔也：如此罢了。［2］圹（kuàng）：同"旷"，旷野。［3］爵：同"雀"。［4］鹯（zhān）：一种像鹞鹰的猛禽。［5］艾：即艾草，常用于灸病，存放时间越久，疗效越好。［6］其何能淑，载胥及溺：引自《诗经·大雅·桑柔》。淑：善，好。载：句首语助词，无义。胥：相。及：与。溺：落水。

【译文】孟子说："夏桀、商纣之所以失去天下，是因为他们失去了民众；之所以失去了民众，是因为他们失去了民心。取得天下有方法：得到民众，就得到了天下；得到民众有方法：

得到他们的心，就得到了民众；得到民众的
心有方法：他们想要的就积蓄起来给他们，
他们憎恶的不强加给他们，如此而已。民众
归依仁德，犹如水往低处流、兽往旷野跑一样。
所以，为渊水驱赶鱼的是水獭，为丛林驱赶
鸟雀的是鹯，为汤王、武王把民众驱赶来的
是夏桀和商纣。如今天下若有喜好仁德的国
君，诸侯们都会为他把民众驱赶过来。即使
不想称王，也不行啊。现今那些要称王天下
的人，就好比患了七年的病要寻求三年的艾
草来医治。假如平时不去积累仁德，是一辈
子也得不到天下的。如果无意于仁政，就会
终身忧患受辱，以致陷入死亡的境地。《诗经》
说：'他们怎么能相处得好，只会相互牵扯
着溺入水中。'就是这个意思。"

【解读】本章孟子谈得天下之法。他用了两个
步骤得以实施，首先是得民，关键是得民心。
得民心，就要顺从民意。得民心者得天下，

失民心者失天下，这是亘古不变的真理。若想得民心，就得施仁政，这是智者的逻辑。在孟子看来，仁政的号召力如同"水之就下、兽之走圹"。落到实处便是想民众之所想，急民众之所急，关注民众生活的基本需要。但为仁政修身积德的事情并非一蹴而就，要有长期的积累，要做好长期的准备。并以"犹七年之病求三年之艾"形容"欲王者"仁德的缺失，深刻形象地反映出当时社会已病入膏肓。仁，是一个社会不可或缺的，仁者爱人，推己及人，这样，社会才会和谐，"欲王者"才会有凝聚力，才不致出现"终身忧辱，以陷于死亡"之危局。

7.10

孟子曰："自暴^[1]者，不可与有言也；
自弃者，不可与有为也。言非^[2]礼义，谓之
自暴也；吾身不能居仁由^[3]义，谓之自弃也。
仁，人之安宅也；义，人之正路也。旷^[4]安
宅而弗居，舍正路而不由，哀哉！"

Mencius said, "With those who do violence
to themselves. it is impossible to speak. With those
who throw themselves away, it is impossible to do
anything. To disown in his conversation propriety
and righteousness, is what we mean by doing
violence to one's self. To say—'I am not able to dwell
in benevolence or pursue the path of righteousness,'
is what we mean by throwing one's self away.
Benevolence is the tranquil habitation of man, and
righteousness is his straight path. Alas for them, who
leave the tranquil dwelling empty and do not reside

in it, and who abandon the right path and do not pursue it!"

【注释】[1] 暴：损害，戕害。[2] 非：诋毁。[3] 由：遵循。[4] 旷：空着。

【注释】孟子说："自己戕害自己的人，同他没有什么可说的；自己抛弃自己的人，同他没有什么可做的。说话诋毁礼义，这叫自己戕害自己；自认为不能守仁行义，这叫自己抛弃自己。仁，是人们最安全的住所；义是人们最正确的道路。空着安全的住所不住，舍弃正确的道路不走，真可悲啊！"

【解读】本章孟子批评自暴自弃者，意在提倡人们应守仁行义。朱熹《四书章句集注》曰："自害其身者，不知礼义之为美而非毁之，虽与之言，必不见信也。自弃其身者，犹知仁义之为美，但溺于怠惰，自谓必不能行，与之

有为必不能勉也。程子曰：'人苟以善自治，
则无不可移者，虽昏愚之至，皆可渐磨而进也。
惟自暴者拒之以不信，自弃者绝之以不为，
虽圣人与居，不能化而入也。'"有的人之
所以会成为自暴自弃者，原因是他们缺乏正
确的人生价值观，不知践行仁义的重要意义。
因此，孟子衷心告诫他们："仁是人们最安
全的住所，义是人们最正确的道路。空着安
全的住所不住，舍弃正确的道路不走，真可
悲啊！"这种人，应该好好温习曾子的话："士
不可以不弘毅，任重而道远。仁以为己任，
不亦重乎？死而后已，不亦远乎？"（《论语·泰
伯》）树立终身践行仁义的人生志向。

7.11

孟子曰："道在迩 [1] 而求诸远，事在易而求诸难。人人亲其亲、长其长而天下平。"

Mencius said, "The path of duty lies in what is near, and men seek for it in what is remote. The work of duty lies in what is easy, and men seek for it in what is difficult. If each man would love his parents and show the due respect to his elders, the whole land would enjoy tranquillity."

【注释】［1］迩：近。

【译文】孟子说："道在近处却往远处寻找，事情原本容易却往难处去做。只要每个人都爱自己的亲人，尊敬自己的长辈，那么天下就会太平。"

【解读】本章孟子讲的是如何理智地践行"道"，"在迩而求诸远""在易而求诸难"都是不明智的做法，凡事不要舍近求远，舍易求难，将简单的问题复杂化是不可取的。实现仁义之道并不难，人人从自身做起，从力所能及的小事做起。每个人都遵循仁义的原则，从孝敬父母、尊敬长辈做起，再延伸到他人（如孟子所说的"老吾老以及人之老，幼吾幼以及人之幼"），天下就太平了。孟子在这里告诉我们，践行道义大可不必好高骛远，把道义看得那么神圣高远，其实"道"就在你身边。

7.12

孟子曰："居下位而不获于上 [1]，民不可得而治也。获于上有道：不信于友，弗获于上矣；信于友有道：事亲弗悦，弗信于友矣；悦亲有道：反身不诚，不悦于亲矣；诚身有道：不明乎善，不诚其身矣。是故诚者，天之道也；思诚者，人之道也。至诚而不动者，未之有也；不诚，未有能动者也。"

Mencius said, "When those occupying inferior situations do not obtain the confidence of the sovereign, they cannot succeed in governing the people. There is a way to obtain the confidence of the sovereign: —if one is not trusted by his friends, he will not obtain the confidence of his sovereign. There is a way of being trusted by one's friends: — if one do not serve his parents so as to make them pleased, he will not be trusted by his friends. There is a way to make one's parents pleased: —if one, on turning his thoughts inwards, finds a want of sincerity, he will not give pleasure to his parents. There is a way to the attainment of sincerity in one's self: —if a man do not understand what is good, he will not attain sincerity in himself. Therefore, sincerity is the way of Heaven. To think how to be sincere is the way of man. Never has there been one possessed of complete sincerity, who did not move others. Never has there been one who had not sincerity who was able to move others."

【注释】 ［1］获于上：得到上级的信任。

【译文】孟子说："职位卑下又得不到上级的信任，是无法治理好百姓的。得到上级的信任有方法：（首先要得到朋友的信任，）假如得不到朋友的信任，则得不到上级的信任；要得到朋友的信任有方法：（首先要得到父母的欢心，）假如侍奉父母而不能够使父母开心，则得不到朋友的信任；要使父母高兴有方法：（首先要诚心诚意，）若是反躬自问，其心不诚，则不能使父母高兴；要做到诚心诚意有方法：（首先应明白什么是善，）若是不明白什么是善，也就无法做到诚心诚意。所以，诚是天的准则，追求诚是做人的准则。有了至诚却不能感动他人的，天下还不曾有过。不诚心，则无法感动他人。"

【解读】本章与《中庸》第二十章中的文字基本相同，只是个别字词有出入。朱熹《四书章句集注》曰："此章述《中庸》孔子之言，见思诚为修身之本，而明善又为思诚之本。"本章的逻辑推理是就人际关系而言的，注重其相连的内转关系：要想取信于上级，就要首先做到取信于朋友；要想取信于朋友，就要首先做到悦亲；要想做到悦亲，就要对父母真诚相待。反过来讲，做到悦亲才能取信于友，做到取信于友才能获得上级的信任。一个对父母都不诚敬的人，很难说他能忠诚于朋友；一个对朋友都不忠诚的人，很难说他能忠诚于上级。总之，"诚"是做人的关键，"诚"也是取信于对方的根本。只有真诚，才能感动别人，才能取信于别人。人际关系是建立在"诚"之上的，一个人如果没有真诚，便无立身之地，故而儒家向来强调"诚"的重要性。

7.13

孟子曰："伯夷辟[1]纣，居北海之滨，闻文王作[2]，兴曰：'盍归乎来[3]！吾闻西伯[4]善养老者。'太公辟纣，居东海之滨，闻文王作，兴曰：'盍归乎来！吾闻西伯善养老者。'二老者，天下之大老也，而归之，是天下之父归之也。天下之父归之，其子焉往？诸侯有行文王之政者，七年之内，必为政于天下矣。"

Mencius said, "Boyi, that he might avoid Zhou, was dwelling on the coast of the northern sea. When he heard of the rise of king Wen, he roused himself, and said, 'Why should I not go and follow him? I have heard that the chief of the West knows well how to nourish the old.' Tai Gong, that he might avoid Zhou, was dwelling on the coast of the eastern sea. When he heard of the rise of king Wen, he roused himself, and said, 'Why should I not go and follow him? I have heard that the chief of the West knows well how to nourish the old.' Those two old men were the greatest old men of the kingdom. When they came to follow king Wen, it was the fathers of the kingdom coming to follow him. When the fathers of the kingdom joined him, how could the sons go to any other? Were any of the princes to practise the government of king Wen, within seven years he would be sure to be giving laws to the kingdom."

【注释】［1］伯夷：殷商时孤竹国君之子。辟：古同"避"，躲避，逃避。［2］作：兴起。［3］盍：副词，相当于"何不"，为什么不。来：语末助词。［4］西伯：即周文王，姬姓，名昌，周太王之孙，季历之子，岐周（今陕西岐山）人。

【译文】孟子说："伯夷为逃避纣王，居住在北海之滨，听说周文王兴起，便说：'为什么不到周文王那里去呢！我听说他是善待老人的人。'姜太公为逃避纣王，居住在东海之滨，听说周文王兴起，便说：'为什么不到周文王那里去呢！我听说他是善待老人的人。'伯夷和太公这两位老者，是天下最有声望的老人，他们都归附周文王，等于天下的老人都到周文王那里去了。天下的老人都归附文王，他们的儿子还能到哪里去呢？诸侯中如果有行文王之政的，七年之内，必定会执政于天下。"

【解读】本章强调了周文王"善养老者"的影响力及所产生的社会效应，并努力呼吁诸侯国有识仁君，趁当前无道之世，赶紧效法文王之政。纣王无道，暴虐臣民，因而臣民逃避；文王施行仁政，关注民生，特别是出台了养老政策，因而民众归服。关于文王"善养老者"，《孟子·尽心上》有述："制其田里，教之树畜，导其妻子，使其养老。"这是我国历史上首次有文献记载的养老制度，伯夷、太公二老的"盍归乎来"，说明了周王朝建立是靠仁政而得天下，是人心所向。周文王的作为正应验了"得民心者得天下，失民心者失天下"。

7.14

孟子曰：“求也为季氏宰[1]，无能改于其德，而赋粟[2]倍他日。孔子曰：'求非我徒也，小子鸣鼓而攻之可也。'由此观之，君不行仁政而富之，皆弃于孔子者也，况于为之强战？争地以战，杀人盈野；争城以战，杀人盈城。此所谓率[3]土地而食人肉，罪不容于死。故善战者服上刑[4]，连[5]诸侯者次之，辟草莱、任土地[6]者次之。”

Mencius said, "Qiu acted as chief officer to the head of the Ji family, whose evil ways he was unable to change, while he exacted from the people double the grain formerly paid. Confucius said, 'He is no disciple of mine. Little children, beat the drum and assail him.' Looking at the subject from this case, we perceive that when a prince was not practising benevolent government, all his ministers who enriched him were rejected by Confucius: —how much more would he have rejected those who are vehement to fight for their prince! When contentions about territory are the ground on which they fight, they slaughter men till the fields are filled with them. When some struggle for a city is the ground on which they fight, they slaughter men till the city is filled with them. This is what is called 'leading on the land to devour human flesh.' Death is not enough for such a crime. Therefore, those who are skilful to fight should suffer the highest punishment. Next to them should be punished those who unite some princes in leagues against others; and next to them, those who take in grassy commons, imposing the cultivation of the ground on the people."

【注释】［1］求：冉求，字子有，孔子学生。季氏：史称"季康子"，春秋时期鲁国的正卿。宰：卿大夫的家臣。［2］赋粟：征收田赋。［3］

率：沿着，循着，此处引申为占领。［4］上刑：重刑。［5］连：联络。［6］辟草莱：开垦土地。莱：草名，同"藜"。任土地：凭依土地征收赋税。

【译文】孟子说："冉求做季康子的家臣，不能改变季康子的德行，反而征收的田赋却增加了一倍。孔子说：'冉求不是我的学生，你们可以大张旗鼓地攻击他。'由此可见，不帮助国君行仁政而去帮他聚敛财富的人，都是被孔子所唾弃的。更何况那些替不仁的国君奋力征战的人呢？他们为争夺土地而战，杀死的人遍野；为争夺城池而战，杀死的人满城，这就是所谓的占土地而吃人肉，死刑都不足以减轻他们的罪过。所以好战的人该受最重的刑罚，从事合纵连横的人该受次一等的刑罚，强令百姓开垦荒地、征收赋税的人受再次一等的刑罚。"

【解读】首先，孟子通过孔子抨击冉求为季康子之家增收赋税的行为，赞扬了孔子的仁政情怀；继而批评那些为争地争城发起战争，导致死伤遍野、死伤满城的罪恶行径。孟子反对盘剥百姓，主张"省刑罚""薄税敛"，减轻民众的负担；更恨不义之战，因为战争大量伤亡的还是百姓。对于发动战争者，他认为判处死刑都不足以抵罪。纵观孟子对战争的看法，他并不反对所有的战争，但对不仁的"争地以战，杀人盈野；争城以战，杀人盈城"极其厌恶，认为这种人与人同类相残，是违反人的崇尚"仁义"向善本性的。与上章对照，文王取得天下，才是"仁义"的体现。人们痛恨战争，然而战争难以避免，世世代代有之，直到今天仍然有之，不仅有，而且因为武器的先进而更加惨烈。因此，和平与发展是当今时代的主题，也是事关全世界各国人民幸福安康的两大问题。反对战争，维护和平。

7.15

孟子曰："存[1]乎人者，莫良于眸子[2]。眸子不能掩其恶。胸中正，则眸子瞭[3]焉；胸中不正，则眸子眊[4]焉。听其言也，观其眸子，人焉廋[5]哉？"

Mencius said, "Of all the parts of a man's body there is none more excellent than the pupil of the eye. The pupil cannot be used to hide a man's wickedness. If within the breast all be correct, the pupil is bright. If within the breast all be not correct, the pupil is dull. Listen to a man's words and look at the pupil of his eye. How can a man conceal his character?"

【注释】［1］存：察，观察。［2］眸子：瞳仁，也指眼睛。［3］瞭：明亮。［4］眊（mào）：朦胧，看不清楚的样子。［5］廋（sōu）：躲藏，隐匿。

【译文】孟子说：“观察一个人，最好莫过于观察他的眼睛。眼睛是不能掩盖人的丑恶的。内心光明正直，眼就明亮；内心不光明正直，眼就昏暗。听一个人说话，要注意观察他的眼睛，他的善恶哪里能藏匿呢？”

【解读】本章孟子从心理学的角度谈观人之法：观察一个人真假善恶，最好看他的眼睛，正应了“眼睛是心灵的窗户”这一名言。孟子善于观察分析人性中的点滴，他发现了人类眼睛的奥秘：一个人在说话的时候，观察他的眼神，可以判断他说的话是真还是假。时至今日，人在说话时，如果心诚话真，就敢与别人坦然相对，眼神就会镇定明亮；如果心虚语假，眼神就会闪躲游离，不敢正视别人，让人感觉眸子“蒙蒙不明”。朱熹在《四书章句集注》中说：“盖人与物接之时，其神在目，故胸中正则神精而明，不正则神散而昏。……言亦心之所发，故并此以观，则人之邪正不可匿矣。然言犹可以伪为，眸子则有不容伪者。"

7.16

孟子曰："恭者不侮人，俭者不夺人。侮夺人之君，惟恐不顺焉，恶得为恭俭？恭俭岂可以声音笑貌为哉？"

Mencius said, "The respectful do not despise others. The economical do not plunder others. The prince who treats men with despite and plunders them, is only afraid that they may not prove obedient to him: —how can he be regarded as respectful or economical? How can respectfulness and economy be made out of tones of the voice, and a smiling manner?"

【译文】孟子说："谦恭的人不会欺侮他人，俭朴的人不会强夺他人。欺侮、强夺的国君，唯恐人们不顺从他，哪里能做到恭敬、俭朴呢？恭敬、俭朴难道是可以用声音和笑脸来做到的吗？”

【解读】本章孟子提出了"恭者""俭者"的为人，"不侮人""不夺人"是道德修养所致，在他们看来，人生而平等，自己并没有什么高贵之处，从不恃才傲物。而那些"侮夺人之君"是难以做到这点的。孟子在这里劝谏执政之君要真诚地做到恭俭，收获了民心，民众自然顺从，根本不用装着笑脸去欺骗民众。总之，还是强调要施行仁政。徐复观说："孟子在政治上谈'仁义'、谈'王道'的具体内容，只是要把政治从以统治者为出发点，以统治者为归结点的方向，彻底扭转过来，使其成为一切为人民而政治。"（《孟子政治思想的基本结构及人治与法治问题》）

7.17

淳于髡[1]曰："男女授受不亲[2]，礼与？"

孟子曰："礼也。"

曰："嫂溺则援[3]之以手乎？"

曰："嫂溺不援，是豺狼也。男女授受不亲，礼也；嫂溺援之以手者，权[4]也。"

曰："今天下溺矣，夫子之不援，何也？"

曰："天下溺，援之以道；嫂溺，援之以手。子欲手援天下乎？"

Chunyu Kun said, "Is it the rule that males and females shall not allow their hands to touch in giving or receiving anything?"

Mencius replied, "It is the rule."

Kun asked, "If a man's sister-in-law be drowning, shall he rescue her with his hand?"

Mencius said, "He who would not so rescue the drowning woman is a wolf. For males and females not to allow their hands to touch in giving and receiving is the general rule; when a sister-in-law is drowning, to rescue her with the hand is a peculiar exigency.' "

Kun said, "The whole kingdom is drowning. How strange it is that you will not rescue it!"

Mencius answered, "A drowning kingdom must be rescued with right principles, as a drowning sister-in-law has to be rescued with the hand. Do you wish me to rescue the kingdom with my hand?"

【注释】［1］淳于髡（kūn）：姓淳于，名髡，齐国政治家、思想家，有名的辩士。［2］男女授受不亲：指男女不能亲手递受物品。授，给予。受，收取。［3］援：牵引，拉。［4］权：权宜，变通。

【译文】淳于髡问："男女之间不亲手递接东西，这是礼吗？"

孟子说:"是礼。"

(淳于髡)又问:"假若嫂嫂掉进水里,可以用手去拉她吗?"

(孟子)说:"嫂嫂掉进水里而不去拉她,这简直是豺狼。男女之间不亲手递接东西,这是正常的礼制;嫂嫂掉进水里用手去拉她,这是变通。"

(淳于髡)说:"如今全天下的人都像掉进水里一样,先生却不去救援,这是为什么呢?"

(孟子)说:"天下的人都掉进水里,要用'道'去救助;嫂嫂掉进水里,要用手去救助,您难道想要我用手去救天下吗?"

【解读】淳于髡不愧为著名辩士,所提问题刁钻,一下子就把孟子置于礼与仁冲突的两难困局:嫂子溺水,你伸手去救吧,违犯了男女授受不亲之礼;你不伸手去救吧,又落了个不仁不义之恶名。孟子机智,果断回敬:"嫂溺不援，是豺狼也！"儒家向来主张"通权达变"，礼，应遵循，但不能拘泥，不能脱离现实、墨守成规，应权衡利弊轻重，灵活运用。继而，又对淳于髡提的第二个问题予以驳斥：面对滔滔乱世，面对陷于水深火热之中的百姓，要用治世方法去援救，哪能用手去援救？我们回顾一下《孟子》以上诸篇，孟子面对梁惠王、齐宣王、滕文公等的劝谏之言，多是治国良策，其以道救天下的拳拳之心，令人感佩。

7.18

公孙丑曰："君子之不教子，何也？"

孟子曰："势不行也。教者必以正[1]；以正不行，继之以怒；继之以怒，则反夷[2]矣。'夫子[3]教我以正，夫子未出于正也。'则是父子相夷也。父子相夷，则恶矣。古者易子而教之。父子之间不责善[4]。责善则离，离则不祥莫大焉。"

Gongsun Chou said, "Why is it that the superior man does not himself teach his son?"

Mencius replied, "The circumstances of the case forbid its being done. The teacher must inculcate what is correct. When he inculcates what is correct, and his lessons are not practised, he follows them up with being angry. When he follows them up with being angry, then, contrary to what should be, he is offended with his son. At the same time, the pupil says, 'My master inculcates on me what is correct, and he himself does not proceed in a correct path.' The result of this is, that father and son are offended with each other. When father and son come to be offended with each other, the case is evil. The ancients exchanged sons, and one taught the son of another. Between father and son, there should be no reproving admonitions to what is good. Such reproofs lead to alienation, and than alienation there is nothing more inauspicious."

【注释】[1]正：正道。[2]夷：伤。[3]夫子：指父亲。[4]责善：劝勉从善。

【译文】公孙丑问："君子不亲自教育子女，这是为什么？"

孟子说："这是因为情势不允许。教育要用正道，正道行不通，接着来的就是愤怒。一旦发怒，反而会伤感情。（子女会说）'您

拿正道教育我，您的行为却不符合正道。'
那么就导致父子之间互相伤害。父子互相伤
害，就不好了。古时候交换子女进行教育，
父子之间不因为劝勉从善而相互责备。劝善
而相互责备，那会导致父子间关系疏远，父
子间关系疏远，没有比这更不好的了。"

【解读】本章讲父子情深不容伤害，应当易子
而教。儒家伦理道德是建立在情感之上的，
以家庭情感为主。孟子认为，在教育方面，
父母教育孩子要使用正确的方式。教育孩子，
孩子不听，父母生气，轻则斥骂，重则拳脚
相加；孩子不服，哭闹反抗，很容易伤害父
子感情。如果因为教育伤害了父子感情，就
失去了教育的本意。易子而教，是古人积累
的经验，自己教育孩子，孩子往往不听，让
别人（老师）去教育，往往使其很顺从。这
样，不但使孩子受到了正确的教育，而且维
护了父子间的亲密情感。如今，如何做父母，

如何做家长，确实是个课题。关于教育，我们都知道有家庭教育、学校教育和社会教育，教育伴随一个人的一生。其中，家庭教育所占的比重最大，孩子除了在学校学习，其他的时间都是跟父母相处，父母是孩子的第一任老师，也是一直陪伴着孩子成长的老师。对父母而言，除了帮助孩子学习知识，还应教会孩子做人的道理，父母的言行举止就是对孩子最好的教育。在培养孩子时，还要讲究方法和沟通方式，做到平等、尊重和理解，促进孩子健康成长。

7.19

孟子曰："事孰为大？事亲为大；守孰
为大？守身为大。不失其身而能事其亲者，
吾闻之矣；失其身而能事其亲者，吾未之闻
也。孰不为事？事亲，事之本也；孰不为守？
守身，守之本也。曾子养曾皙[1]，必有酒肉。
将彻[2]，必请所与。问有余，必曰'有'。
曾皙死，曾元[3]养曾子，必有酒肉。将彻，
不请所与。问有余，曰'亡矣'。将以复进也，
此所谓养口体者也。若曾子，则可谓养志也。
事亲若曾子者，可也。"

Mencius said, "Of services, which is the
greatest? The service of parents is the greatest. Of
charges, which is the greatest? The charge of one's
self is the greatest. That those who do not fail to
keep themselves are able to serve their parents is
what I have heard. But I have never heard of any,

who, having failed to keep themselves, were able notwithstanding to serve their parents. There are many services, but the service of parents is the root of all others. There are many charges, but the charge of one's self is the root of all others. The philosopher Zeng, in nourishing Zeng Xi, was always sure to have wine and flesh provided. And when they were being removed, he would ask respectfully to whom he should give what was left. If his father asked whether there was anything left, he was sure to say, 'There is.' After the death of Zeng Xi, when Zeng Yuan came to nourish Zengzi, he was always sure to have wine and flesh provided. But when the things were being removed, he did not ask to whom he should give what was left, and if his father asked whether there was anything left, he would answer 'No,' —intending to bring them in again. This was what is called— 'nourishing the mouth and body.' We may call Zengzi's practice— 'nourishing the will.' To serve one's parents as Zengzi served his, may be accepted as filial piety."

【注释】［1］曾皙：曾子之父，孔子早期的学生。［2］彻：撤除，撤去。［3］曾元：曾参之子。

【译文】孟子说："侍奉谁最重要？侍奉父母最重要；守护什么最重要？守护自身的节操最重要。不失去自身的节操而又能够侍奉好父母的，我听说过；失去节操而能侍奉好父母的，我没有听说过。谁不该侍奉？该侍奉的很多，但侍奉父母是根本。什么不该守护？该守护的很多，但守护自身的节操是根本。曾子奉养其父曾皙，每顿饭必定有酒肉。撤席时，一定要请示剩下的给谁。曾皙若问是否还有剩余，一定要说'有'。曾皙死，曾元奉养曾子，每餐必有酒肉。撤席时，曾元便不请示剩下的给谁。曾子若问是否还有剩余，便回答说'没有了'。然后将剩余的到下顿饭时重新呈上。曾元的这种养，只能叫作养身。像曾子的这种养，才可叫作养心。侍奉父母像曾子这样，就可以了。"

【解读】本章孟子阐述了"事亲"与"守身"的内涵及其关系，他认为，尽孝道要守身和事亲，守护住自己的品行节操，才能侍奉好父母。《孝经》里说："身体发肤，受之父母，不敢毁伤，孝之始也。"自己的身体是父母生命在我们身上的延续，我们要保护好自己的身体，不让它受到损害；不仅守护好身体，还要守护好节操，否则，让自身陷入不忠不仁不义的境地，就会牵连父母受到侮辱，这就是不孝。这里孟子还强调，侍奉父母不仅能要"养身"，还要"养志"。孔子说："今之孝者，是谓能养。至于犬马，皆能有养，不敬，何以别乎！"（《论语·为政》）对待老人，只做到养不行，还要做到敬，做不到敬，则与犬马牲畜无别。只有做到敬，老人才心情舒畅。曾子遵循孔子的教诲，提出"大孝尊亲，其次不辱，其下能养"（《大戴礼记·曾子大孝》），认为做到"尊亲"是大孝，做到不辱没父母、不给父母落骂名是次一等的孝，只做到养（"养"是孝的底线）是下等的孝。曾元侍奉曾参时，只满足他的口腹之需，不考虑他的精神需要，甚至欺骗他，这只是养身，属于下等的孝。孟子强调，要向曾参学习，侍奉老人时，不只是做到养身，还要做到养志。

7.20

孟子曰："人不足与適 [1] 也，政不足间 [2] 也。惟大人为能格 [3] 君心之非。君仁莫不仁，君义莫不义，君正莫不正。一正君而国定矣。"

Mencius said, "It is not enough to remonstrate with a sovereign on account of the mal-employment of ministers, nor to blame errors of government. It is only the great man who can rectify what is wrong in the sovereign's mind. Let the prince be benevolent, and all his acts will be benevolent. Let the prince be righteous, and all his acts will be righteous. Let the prince be correct, and everything will be correct. Once rectify the ruler, and the kingdom will be firmly settled."

【注释】［1］適：通"谪"，谴责，责备。［2］间（jiàn）：非议。［3］大人：指德行高尚、志趣高远的人。格：纠正，匡正。

【译文】孟子说："当政的小人不值得去责备，他们的政事也不值得去非议。只有大德之人才能够匡正国君不正确的言行。如果国君仁爱，那么没有人不仁爱；如果国君正义，那么没有人不正义；如果国君端正，那么没有人不端正。国君端正了，那么国家也就安定了。"

【解读】孟子在本章提出了"格君心之非"这一概念，这是儒家一贯主张的政治理念。"人非圣贤，孰能无过"，在人治社会，只有君主拥有绝对的权力，那些当政的小人言行会影响君主，按照各尽其责的原则，如果君主有了错误倾向，其政令关乎国家的兴废存亡，所以，孟子认为只有那些大德之人，才勇于担当，站出来敢于谏言，匡正国君不正确的想法和做法。孟子曾言："我先攻其邪心，心既正，而后天下之事可从而理也。"（朱熹《四书章句集注》）像孔子，面对鲁、齐、卫诸国国君敢于规劝，孟子面对梁惠王、齐宣王、滕文公勇于谏言。他们的劝谏，很大程度上起到了"格君心之非"的作用。同时，孟子还强调君王的表率作用，君仁民就仁，君义民就义，君正民就正，这与孔子所说的"君子之德风，小人之德草。草上之风，必偃"（《论语·颜渊》）是一个道理。

7.21

孟子曰："有不虞[1]之誉，有求全之毁。"

Mencius said, "There are cases of praise which could not be expected, and of reproach when the parties have been seeking to be perfect."

【注释】[1]虞：预料，意想。

【译文】孟子说："有意想不到的赞誉，也有苛求完美的诋毁。"

【解读】本章孟子提出面对"不虞之誉"与"求全之毁"的人生态度，考验着人的人格定力。人生在世，毁誉常存，遇誉勿喜，遇毁勿悲，做到如此，要有修己功夫。做人不要被世俗所累，不以物喜，不以己悲，不违背自然规律，不去强求外物，不去强人所难，不去不择手段地追求物质利益，而要加强道德修养，保持乐观心态。人要重视内在修养，修养达到一定程度，水到渠成，名也好，利也罢，都是顺其自然的事情。

7.22

孟子曰：“人之易^[1]其言也，无责^[2]耳矣。”

Mencius said, "Men's being ready with their tongues arises simply from their not having been reproved."

【注释】［1］易：轻易。［2］无责：无责任心。

【译文】孟子说：“人说话轻率，说明他无责任心罢了。”

【解读】孟子认为，说话轻率是没有责任心的表现。人应该有责任心，应该慎言，应该说到做到，不要信口开河，只说空话，不干实事。这方面，孔子曾强调学习古人：“古者言之不出，耻躬之不逮也。”（《论语·里仁》）古时人的话不轻易出口，是怕自身做不到而感到羞耻。并强调："君子欲讷于言而敏于行。"（《论语·里仁》）君子要在说话上谨慎迟钝，而在做事上勤快敏捷。要用君子人格要求自己，要对自己的言语负责，说出去的话就像泼出去的水，我们都知道覆水难收这个道理。

7.23

孟子曰：“人之患在好为人师。”

Mencius said, "The evil of men is that they like to be teachers of others."

【译文】孟子说：“一些人的毛病就在于喜欢当别人的老师。”

【解读】“好为人师”，按说不是缺点，孟子为何视为“毛病”呢？这是因为此话有着特指性，有些好为人师者，不具备为人师的资格，学识水平欠缺，却自满自大，自以为是，不谦不恭，不懂装懂。这种人，古今皆有之，他们既有害于受教者，也有毁于自身形象。因而要求，为人师者要有渊博的学问和谦逊的品德，自己的知识和能力要得到大家的认可，然后方能帮助别人解惑答疑，指点人生的困惑。

孟子曰
人之患
在好為
人師

庚午年
楊沙剛
敬繪

人之患在好为人师　杨晓刚　绘

7.24

乐正子从于子敖^[1]之齐。

乐正子见孟子。孟子曰："子亦来见我乎？"

曰："先生何为出此言也？"

曰："子来几日矣？"

曰："昔者^[2]。"

曰："昔者，则我出此言也，不亦宜乎？"

曰："舍馆未定。"

曰："子闻之也，舍馆定，然后求见长者乎？"

曰："克有罪。"

The disciple Yue Zheng went in the train of Zi-ao to Qi.

He came to see Mencius, who said to him, "Do you also come to see me?"

Yuezheng replied, "Master, why do you speak

such words?"

"How many days have you been here?" asked Mencius.

"I came yesterday."

"Yesterday! Is it not with reason then that I thus speak?"

"My lodging-house was not arranged."

"Have you heard that a scholar's lodging-house must be arranged before he visits his elder?"

Yuezheng said, "I have done wrong."

【注释】［1］乐正子：鲁人，名克，孟子弟子。子敖：即王驩，字子敖，齐王宠臣。［2］昔者：昨天。

【译文】乐正子跟随子敖来到齐国。

乐正子拜见孟子。孟子问："你也来见我吗？"

（乐正子）答："先生为什么说出这样

的话呢？"

（孟子）问："你来几天了？"

（乐正子）答："昨天才来。"

（孟子）问："昨天啊，那我说这样的话，不合适吗？"

（乐正子）答："是因为住的舍馆没有定下来。"

（孟子）问："那你听说过，舍馆定下后，才去拜见长辈的吗？"

（乐正子）答："是我有过错。"

【解读】此章通过孟子与学生乐正子的对话，看似向人们展示了师生相处之道，其实是事出有因。孟子曾与王驩一起出使过滕国，孟子为正，王驩为副，王驩自恃得宠，代替孟子包办了一切，孟子了解了他的为人，因此心怀不满。孟子本就不屑与王驩为伍，而弟子乐正子却跟这样的人在一起，自然心里感到对弟子的成长极为不利。因此，孟子抓住乐正子没有及时拜见老师这一过错，对其进行了旁敲侧击。乐正子感悟到了自己的错误：不应与德行差的人为伍，不应轻慢了尊师之道，因此，赶紧向老师诚恳道歉。这也反映出乐正子知错即改的优良品质。

7.25

孟子谓乐正子曰："子之从于子敖来，
徒饣甫啜[1]也。我不意子学古之道，而以饣甫啜也。"

Mencius, addressing the disciple Yuezheng,
said to him, "Your coming here in the train of Zi-
ao was only because of the food and the drink. I
could not have thought that you, having learned the
doctrine of the ancients, would have acted with a
view to eating and drinking."

【注释】［1］饣甫（bù）：吃。啜：喝。

【译文】孟子对乐正子说："你这次跟随子敖来，
只为吃喝呀。我不希望你学习古人之道，只
是用来混吃混喝。"

【解读】接上章，孟子对乐正子继续点拨，指明人生道路。孟子认为，乐正子学古之道只是为了跟随王驩混吃混喝，有辱平生所学，忘记了学道的本意。孟子这么批评的用意，是教诲弟子做一些有意义的事，实现人生价值。人活着，只知道吃喝玩乐，无异于酒囊饭袋和行尸走肉。人活着，要体现自我价值，做对社会有用的人。正是孟子的这种点滴之教，才有了闻"鲁欲使乐正子为政"而"喜而不寐"（《孟子·告子下》）的结果。

7.26

孟子曰："不孝有三，无后为大。舜不告而娶，为无后也，君子以为犹告也。"

Mencius said, "There are three things which are unfilial, and to have no posterity is the greatest of them. Shun married without informing his parents because of this, lest he should have no posterity. Superior men consider that his doing so was the same as if he had informed them."

【译文】孟子说："不孝的情况有三种，尤以没有后代最为严重。舜没有禀告父母就娶妻，为的就是怕没有后代。所以君子认为他虽然没有禀告也和禀告了一样。"

【解读】本章讲孝道。朱熹《四书章句集注》引赵岐注曰："于礼有不孝者三事：谓阿意曲从，陷亲不义，一也；家贫亲老，不为禄仕，二也；不娶无子，绝先祖祀，三也。三者之中，无后为大。""无后为大"，这是古人的观念，孟子在此抛出这一观点，并以舜"不告而娶"加以说明，有其历史的局限性。从实际来看，有无子嗣，并非以人的意志为定，而是由人的生理条件、客观因素所决定。因此，不能说生不出儿子就是最大的不孝，这是重男轻女的不良世俗观念。

7.27

　　孟子曰："仁之实，事亲是也；义之实，从兄是也；智之实，知斯二者弗去是也；礼之实，节文[1]斯二者是也；乐之实，乐斯二者，乐则生矣，生则恶可已[2]也，恶可已，则不知足之蹈之、手之舞之。"

Mencius said. "The richest fruit of benevolence is this: —the service of one's parents. The richest fruit of righteousness is this: —the obeying one's elder brothers. The richest fruit of wisdom is this: —the knowing those two things, and not departing from them. The richest fruit of propriety is this: —the ordering and adorning those two things. The richest fruit of music is this: —the rejoicing in those two things. When they are rejoiced in, they grow. Growing, how can they be repressed? When they come to this state that they cannot be repressed, then unconsciously the feet begin to dance and the hands to move."

【注释】［1］节：调节。文：修饰。［2］已：停止。

【译文】孟子说："仁的实质，是侍奉父母；义的实质，是顺从兄长；智的实质，是懂得这两者而不背离；礼的实质，是对这两者进行合理地调节修饰；乐的实质，是喜欢这两者，于是快乐就自然产生，快乐一产生就消除了厌恶情绪，（快乐）抑制不住，就会不知不觉地手舞足蹈起来。"

【解读】本章孟子讲仁义智礼乐的实质及其关系。仁的本质是孝，义的本质是悌，智的本质是知晓仁义，礼的本质是规范仁义，乐的本质是乐在仁义。张岱年在《中国哲学大纲》中说："孟子哲学的中心观念则是仁义。"

仁义是孟子思想的核心，礼智乐都围绕着仁义展开。孝敬父母，尊敬长辈，维护浓浓的亲情，是仁义的根本。这一根本，经过礼的规范，乐的调节修饰，达到完美，人人喜爱，人人践行。朱熹《四书章句集注》曰："此章言事亲从兄，良心真切，天下之道，皆原于此。然必知之明而守之固，然后节之密而乐之深也。"理解此章，不要认为孟子的仁爱只是局限于父兄亲情，还要结合孟子"老吾老以及人之老，幼吾幼以及人之幼"等言论全面地看待。把仁爱父兄之情推而广之，就可达到兼爱天下之境界。

7.28

孟子曰："天下大悦而将归己，视天下悦而归己，犹草芥也，惟舜为然。不得乎亲，不可以为人；不顺乎亲，不可以为子。舜尽事亲之道而瞽瞍厎豫 [1]，瞽瞍厎豫而天下化，瞽瞍厎豫而天下之为父子者定，此之谓大孝。"

Mencius said, "Suppose the case of the whole kingdom turning in great delight to an individual to submit to him. To regard the whole kingdom thus turning to him in great delight but as a bundle of grass; — only Shun was capable of this. He considered that if one could not get the hearts of his parents, he could not be considered a man, and that if he could not get to an entire accord with his parents, he could not be considered a son. By Shun's completely fulfilling everything by which a parent could be served, Gusou was brought to find delight in what was good. When Gusou was brought to find that delight, the whole kingdom was transformed. When Gusou was brought to find that delight, all fathers and sons in the kingdom were established in their respective duties. This is called great filial piety."

【注释】〔1〕底（zhǐ）豫：得到欢乐。底，致。豫，乐。

【译文】孟子说："天下人都非常高兴地要来归顺自己，把天下人高兴地要来归顺自己看得如同草芥一般，只有舜是这样。不能使父母欢心，不可以为人；不顺从父母的心意，不可以为子。舜尽心侍奉双亲，使父亲瞽瞍由不高兴到高兴；瞽瞍高兴了进而天下的人受到了感化；使瞽瞍高兴了，天下父子间的伦常规范也就确定了，这就叫作大孝。"

【解读】孟子以舜为孝道典范，强调大孝精神的作用。在孟子看来，舜把天下归依看作是一种极其自然的现象，只要自己具备了仁德，百姓自然而然被其吸引。同时我们应该注意，舜也没有把天下归依当作最大的快乐，而是以能尽心事亲作为最高追求并以此为乐、乐此不疲。上章阐述了仁义智礼乐的实质，其根本在于"孝"，天下归依的基本动力在于一个"孝"字。孝是仁的表现，舜之孝，实为仁也。舜的孝行给天下人做出了表率，所以孟子言"瞽瞍底豫而天下之为父子者定"。只有天下事亲，才能天下归仁，只有天下归仁，才能天下归心。

离娄下

Li Lou 2

8.1

孟子曰："舜生于诸冯[1]，迁于负夏，卒于鸣条，东夷之人也。文王生于岐周[2]，卒于毕郢[3]，西夷之人也。地之相去也，千有余里；世之相后也，千有余岁。得志行乎中国，若合符节[4]。先圣后圣，其揆[5]一也。"

Mencius said, "Shun was born in Zhufeng, removed to Fuxia, and died in Mingtiao; —a man near the wild tribes on the east. King Wen was born in Zhou by mount Qi, and died in Biying; — a man near the wild tribes on the west. Those regions were distant from one another more than a thousand *li*, and the age of the one sage was posterior to that of the other more than a thousand years. But when they got their wish, and carried their principles into practice throughout the Middle Kingdom, it was like uniting the two halves of a seal. When we examine

孟
子

those sages, both the earlier and the later, their principles are found to be the same."

【注释】［1］诸冯：地名，传说在今山东菏泽南五十里。一说在山西。［2］岐周：岐山下周的旧邑，在今陕西岐山县东北。［3］毕郢：在今陕西咸阳市东。［4］符节：信物。［5］揆：尺度，准则。

【译文】孟子说："舜出生在诸冯，迁居到负夏，死在鸣条，是东部民族的人。周文王出生在岐周，死在毕郢，是西部民族的人。两地相距一千多里，时代相隔一千多年。但他们得志后在中国推行的治国之道，就像有信物一样吻合。前代的圣人和后代的圣人，他们所遵循的准则是一样的。"

【解读】本章所言舜与文王，皆是儒家眼里贤明的帝王形象，他们虽然在空间上和时间上

254

相距甚远，面对的社会形态也大不相同，但其治下的社会都成了后世"心向往之"的理想国度。究其根本，全赖于他们一致的治国之道：明礼重孝，施行仁政，爱护百姓。换句话说，文王正是由于继承和发扬了舜的治国之道，才最终取得了和舜一样的成就。由此可以看出，孟子在这里是要借助历史经验告诫当时的统治者：若想治理好国家，就要向舜和文王那样的帝王学习，施仁政，爱百姓。今时今日，这个道理依然适用，我们一方面要继承历史上优秀的管理理念，另一方面还要在此基础上改革创新，这样我们的管理水平和治理能力才能不断提高，我们的国家和社会才能不断进步。

8.2

子产听郑国之政，以其乘舆济人于溱、
洧[1]。孟子曰："惠[2]而不知为政。岁十一
月徒杠[3]成，十二月舆梁[4]成，民未病涉也。
君子平其政，行辟[5]人可也，焉得人人而济
之？故为政者，每人而悦之，日亦不足矣。"

When Zichan was chief minister of the state
of Zheng, he would convey people across the Zhen
and Wei in his own carriage. Mencius said, "It was
kind, but showed that he did not understand the
practice of government. When in the eleventh month
of the year the foot-bridges are completed, and the
carriage-bridges in the twelfth month, the people
have not the trouble of wading. Let a governor
conduct his rule on principles of equal justice, and,
when he goes abroad, he may cause people to be
removed out of his path. But how can he convey

子产以其乘舆济人于溱、洧　岳海波　绘

everybody across the rivers? It follows that if a governor will try to please everybody, he will find the days not surficient for his work."

【注释】［1］溱（zhēn）、洧（wěi）：皆水名，在今河南省。［2］惠：小利。［3］徒杠：简易的独木桥。［4］舆梁：可通行马车的大桥。［5］辟：通"避"，回避，避让。

【译文】郑国大夫子产执掌国政，用自己乘坐的车子帮人们渡过溱河与洧河。孟子评论说："子产仁惠却不懂得处理政事。如果在十一月把行人的小桥建好，十二月把行车的大桥建好，那么百姓就不会为过河发愁。君子处理好了政务，出行时让人们回避也是可以的，哪能一个一个地去帮行人渡河呢？所以管理国政的人，想取悦于每个人，时间是不够用的。"

【解读】子产在郑国为相期间多有建树，连孔子都赞其"有君子之道四焉：其行己也恭，其事上也敬，其养民也惠，其使民也义"（《论语·公冶长》）。然而孟子在本章却说他"惠而不知为政"，这是何故？其实二者并不矛盾，孔子是对子产一生德行的总体性评价，是论人；而孟子则是就子产"以其乘舆济人于溱、洧"这件事的评论，是论事。孟子在这里强调，为政者应"在其位，谋其政"，子产身居要职，应该胸怀全局，谋划大事，施行仁政，从根本上解决普遍性的民生大问题，而不应该忙忙碌碌地去施行小惠。这对我们树立治国理政的大局观，具有一定的启发意义。

8.3

孟子告齐宣王曰："君之视臣如手足，则臣视君如腹心；君之视臣如犬马，则臣视君如国人；君之视臣如土芥 [1]，则臣视君如寇仇 [2]。"

王曰："礼，为旧君有服 [3]，何如斯可为服矣？"

曰："谏行言听，膏泽下于民；有故而去，则君使人导之出疆，又先 [4] 于其所往；去三年不反，然后收其田里。此之谓三有礼焉。如此，则为之服矣。今也为臣，谏则不行，言则不听；膏泽不下于民；有故而去，则君搏执 [5] 之，又极 [6] 之于其所往；去之日，遂收其田里。此之谓寇仇。寇仇何服之有？"

Mencius said to the king Xuan of Qi, "When the prince regards his ministers as his hands and feet, his ministers regard their prince as their belly and heart; when he regards them as his dogs and horses, they regard him as another man; when he regards them as the ground or as grass, they regard him as a robber and an enemy."

The king said, "According to the rules of propriety, a minister wears mourning when he has left the service of a prince. How must a prince behave that his old ministers may thus go into mourning?"

Mencius replied, "The admonitions of a minister having been followed, and his advice listened to, so that blessings have descended on the people, if for some cause he leaves the country, the prince sends an escort to conduct him beyond the boundaries. He also anticipates with recommendatory intimations his arrival in the country to which he is proceeding. When he has been gone three years and does not return, only then at length does he take back his fields and residence.

This treatment is what is called a 'thrice-repeated display of consideration.' When a prince acts thus, mourning will be worn on leaving his service. Nowadays, the remonstrances of a minister are not followed, and his advice is not listened to, so that no blessings descend on the people. When for any cause he leaves the country, the prince tries to seize him and hold him a prisoner. He also pushes him to extremity in the country to which he has gone, and on the very day of his departure, takes back his fields and residence. This treatment shows him to be what we call 'a robber and an enemy.' What mourning can be worn for a robber and an enemy?"

【注释】［1］土：泥土。芥：小草。［2］寇仇：仇敌。［3］服：丧服，此处为服丧之意。［4］先：使人先去安排布置。［5］搏执：拘捕。［6］极：使之穷困。

【译文】孟子对齐宣王说："君主把臣下视为手足，臣下就会把君主当作腹心对待；君主把臣下视为狗马，臣下就会把君主当作一般人对待；君主把臣下视为泥土草芥，臣下就会把君主当作仇敌对待。"

齐宣王说："礼制规定，已经离职的臣下也应为过去的国君服丧。国君怎样做，臣下才会为其服丧呢？"

（孟子）说："臣下在职时有谏言，君主采纳，使君主恩泽施及民众；臣下因故要离开国家时，君主派人引导他出境，并派人先到他要去的地方做好安排；离去了三年还不回来，才收回他的土地和房屋。这就叫作三有礼。国君如果这样做了，臣下就会为他服丧。如今做臣下的，他们的劝谏，君王不接受，他们的建议，君王不采纳；恩泽不能施及百姓；臣下因故要离开，君主就拘捕他，他去到一个地方，君主就想方设法使其穷困；并在臣下离开的当天就收回他的土地和房屋。这就叫作仇敌。对待像仇敌一样的国君，还服什么丧呢？"

【解读】孔子曾说："君使臣以礼，臣事君以忠。"
（《论语·八佾》）儒家认为，君与臣在地
位上虽有高低之分，但二者的关系应是建立
在情感和道义基础上的，应是一种良性的互
动关系，若要臣民忠诚，君王首先就要以礼
相待。孟子在本章开篇便以语势强烈的排比
句提醒齐宣王：只有真诚地对待、关爱臣民，
臣民才会对君王竭尽忠心；反之，臣民就会
与君王离心离德，甚至反目成仇。紧接着，
孟子又从正反两方面进行对比，强调了君臣
之间的理想关系：君王"三有礼"，臣民"可
为服"。因此，我们可以得出这样的结论：
君臣之间的关系如何，很大程度上取决于君
王对待臣民的态度。需要注意的是，孟子的
这一思想与后世儒"君要臣死，臣不得不死"
的主张并不是一以贯之的，足以说明先秦儒
家并不提倡愚忠。

孟子与齐宣王论辩　韩新维　绘

8.4

孟子曰："无罪而杀士，则大夫可以去；
无罪而戮民，则士可以徙。"

Mencius said, "When scholars are put to death
without any crime, the great officers may leave the
country. When the people are slaughtered without
any crime, the scholars may remove."

【译文】孟子说："没有罪过却随便杀害士人，
那么做大夫的就可以考虑辞官而去；没有罪
过就随便杀害百姓，那么士人就可以考虑迁
徙。"

【解读】在孟子生活的时代，士是学习、传播
圣贤之道的读书人，大夫是统治者发布政策
和指令的具体实施者。如果士无辜被杀，就
说明统治者背离了圣贤之道，在这种情况下，

大夫还要执行错误政令的话，无异于助纣为虐。因此，面对暴君，有正义感的大夫选择离开，才是明智之举。同理，统治者滥杀无辜百姓，则说明圣贤之道在这里难以推行，有正义感的士当然要选择迁居别处。孟子在本章意在向统治者强调：施行暴政，滥杀无辜，必将众叛亲离。当然，孟子在这里没有去无可去，徙无处可徙的终极追问与思考。

8.5

孟子曰："君仁莫不仁，君义莫不义。"

Mencius said, "If the sovereign be benevolent, all will be benevolent. If the sovereign be righteous, all will be righteous."

【译文】孟子说："君王仁爱就没有人不仁爱，君王讲义就没有人不讲义。"

【解读】上一章说的是统治者"不仁"的危害性，本章接着从正面讲统治者"仁"的重要性。统治者施行仁政，百姓就会拥戴，政权方能稳固。施行仁政的前提是统治者自身必须具备极高的道德修养水平，然后上行下效。孟子在这里完全继承孔子"君子之德风，小人之德草。草上之风，必偃"（《论语·颜渊》）的衣钵。

8.6

孟子曰："非礼之礼，非义之义，大人弗为。"

Mencius said, "Acts of propriety which are not really proper, and acts of righteousness which are not really righteous, the great man does not do."

【译文】孟子说："不符合礼制的礼，不符合道义的义，德行高尚的人是不会去做的。"

【解读】儒家认为，"礼"是建立在一定秩序之上的礼仪规范，"义"是以道德为基础的相宜的行为准则。有些行为在形式上看是合乎礼、义的，在实质上却违背了礼、义。比如，《论语·八佾》里提到的季氏，身为大夫，却僭用天子的八佾之舞，被孔子怒斥为"是可忍也，孰不可忍也"（《论语·八佾》）；还有"巧言、令色、足恭（过分地恭敬）"者，被孔子批评为"左丘明耻之，丘亦耻之"（《论语·公冶长》），这就是"非礼之礼"。有些人，为了所谓的朋友情谊没有原则，不讲规矩，充其量算痞气十足的"江湖义气"，这就是"非义之义"。孟子在本章强调：是君子，就要诚意、正心地去践行礼、义，不要做徒有其表的表演。

8.7

孟子曰："中也养不中[1]，才也养不才，故人乐有贤父兄也。如中也弃不中，才也弃不才，则贤不肖之相去，其间不能以寸[2]。"

Mencius said, "Those who keep the Mean, train up those who do not, and those who have abilities, train up those who have not, and hence men rejoice in having fathers and elder brothers who are possessed of virtue and talent. If they who keep the Mean spurn those who do not, and they who have abilities spurn those who have not, then the space between them—those so gifted and the ungifted—will not admit an inch."

【注释】［1］中：朱熹《四书章句集注》："无过不及之谓中。"养：朱熹注为"谓涵育熏陶，俟其自化也"。［2］其间不能以寸：其间不能以寸量，指相差无几。

【译文】孟子说："有德行的中正之人能够教育培养德行有偏邪的人，有才能的人能够教育培养没才能的人，因此人们喜欢自己有德才的父兄长辈。如果有德行的中正之人放弃偏邪无德行的人，有才能的人放弃没才能的人，那么贤能的人和不贤能的人之间的差距，就不能用分寸来计量了。"

【解读】在儒家眼里，世间万物都可以被化育，人更不例外。一个没有德行和才华的人，固然可以通过自己的努力去修养道德、修炼本领，但同样离不开有德有才之人的教育、熏陶和帮助，在他们的指点下，"不中""不才"者就会少走弯路，快速提高。所以人们都希望自己的父兄就是这样的贤德之人，以便沐其春风之育。但是，如果有德有才者选择孤芳自赏，甚至放弃对后进者教育的话，那么也就不能把他看作是有贤德的中正之人了。

本章意在强调：有德才者要承担起自己的社会责任，帮助没有德才的人，形成良好的社会风气。

8.8

孟子曰："人有不为也，而后可以有为。"

Mencius said, "Men must be decided on what they will NOT do, and then they are able to act with vigour in what they ought to do."

【译文】孟子说："人要懂得有所不为，然后才能有所作为。"

【解读】人生在世，谁不想大有作为，青史留名？奈何世事繁杂，生命有限。若想在有限的时间里取得一番成就，人们首先要认清自己，量力而行，并在此基础上学会选择与舍弃，果断舍弃那些力不能任的事情，然后选择适合自己的事业全力以赴，不虚度、不旁骛。当然，人们在选择的时候必须遵守一定的原则。这个原则就是"义字当先"，不合道义的，于国家、百姓有害的，要坚决"不为"；合乎道义的，对国家、百姓有利的，要果断"有为"。在各种诱惑铺天盖地而来的今天，我们每个人都应学会取舍，坚守底线，明确哪些事"不为"，然后才能在广阔的天地里"有为"。

8.9

孟子曰："言人之不善，当如后患何？"

Mencius said, "What future misery have they and ought they to endure, who talk of what is not good in others!"

【译文】孟子说："议论别人不好的地方，由此引起的后患该怎么办呢？"

【解读】常言道："静坐常思己过，闲谈莫论人非。"不在背后议论别人的是非，或者宣扬他人的缺点，这是君子的基本素质。如果对方有不足，完全可以用恰当的方式当面指出，帮助他改正；也可以以此为鉴，反省自身，有则改之，无则加勉，这才是君子所为。此外，不"言人之不善"也是君子处世的一种智慧。喜欢挑人毛病、揭人之短的人，一定会因为自己的不当行为祸及自身，轻则陷于口舌之争，重则遭受皮肉之苦。果真如此，岂不是搬起石头砸了自己的脚吗？因此，孟子在本章告诉人们一定要谨慎言行。

8.10

孟子曰："仲尼不为已甚者。"

Mencius said, "Zhongni did not do extraordinary things."

【译文】孟子说："孔子待人处事从不做过分的事。"

【解读】本章以孔子为例，讲的是儒家推崇的中庸之道。"中庸"是儒家的一种处世智慧，它要求人们做到"无过无不及"，把握好适度原则。同时，"中庸"被孔子称为"至德"，是君子在道德修养层面需要达到的境界。君子必须具备"仁"和"知"两个要素，"仁"是先天即有的德行基础，"知"是经后天学习而明确的道德修养方向，将二者集于己身，便能沿着孔子的方向臻于道德之化境。

8.11

孟子曰："大人者，言不必信，行不必果，惟义所在。"

Mencius said, "The great man does not think beforehand of his words that they may be sincere, nor of his actions that they may be resolute; —he simply speaks and does what is right."

【译文】孟子说："有德行的人，说话不一定句句讲信用，做事情不一定非要有结果，只要合乎道义就可以。"

【解读】诚信是中华民族的传统美德，本章却说"言不必信"，难道是孟子要冒天下之大不韪吗？当然不是。本章所言体现了孟子在君子修身与处世问题上的辩证思想：修身养性时，主观能动性占据主导，言而有信自然是君子要坚守的美德；为人处世时，事情就会变得复杂起来，需要考虑客观因素，诚信就不再是第一选项。此时君子就要学会变通，而变通则应遵循"惟义所在"的原则，即要做到"以义为先"。尾生守信，抱柱而死。明知己错，却要顽固坚持，这类不知灵活变通者被孔子喻为"硁硁然小人哉"（《论语·子路》）。之所以称其为小人，是因为他们坚守的事情没价值，不符合大义。古往今来，中国从来不缺坚守大义的"大人者"，他们为了民族大义，勇于奋斗，不拘小节，甚至不惜背负骂名，但最终无一不成为鲁迅先生称赞的"中国的脊梁"。

8.12

孟子曰："大人者，不失其赤子[1]之心者也。"

Mencius said, "The great man is he who does not lose his child's heart."

【注释】［1］赤子：婴儿。

【译文】孟子说："德行高尚的人，是不失童贞之心的人。"

【解读】孟子在本章以"赤子之心"比喻君子与生俱来、矢志不渝的美好品德。不管世事如何纷扰，君子始终保有真诚纯洁、乐观善良的本心。他们远离世俗欲望，摒除私心杂念，胸怀天下，仁而爱人，克己复礼，循义而行。纵使前路漫漫、荆棘遍地，君子也从未"失其赤子之心",因为初心洁白无瑕,所以他们能心无旁骛,勇往直前。今天,"不忘初心"已成为党员干部乃至各行各业频繁提到的"热词"。"不忘初心"是对历史规律和时代潮流的自觉遵循;"不忘初心"才不会迷失自我、随波逐流,人格才会散发出恒久的魅力。

孟子曰大人者不失其赤子
之心者也 藏之庚子初春月
吴磊於浪瑑

赤子之心　吴磊　绘

8.13

孟子曰："养生者不足以当大事，惟送死可以当大事。"

Mencius said, "The nourishment of parents when living is not sufficient to be accounted the great thing. It is only in the performing their obsequies when dead that we have what can be considered the great thing."

【译文】孟子说："父母活着的时候赡养他们称不上大事，他们去世后安葬他们才可以称得上是大事。"

【解读】儒家认为，父母在世之时，人们自然要去赡养他们，这是人之常情，也是孝道的应有之义，不能算作"大事"；然而，父母的离世却是人们生活中遭遇的重大变故，这也几乎是子女最后一次尽孝的机会，并且在葬、祭过程中事事都要出于诚心、合乎礼仪，因此，这当然要视作"大事"。古时乃至当今，人们一直将"婚、丧、嫁、娶"视为大事，孔子曾说："所重：民、食、丧、祭。"（《论语·尧曰》）"丧事不敢不勉。"（《论语·子罕》）这并非轻养重葬，而是要求人们对"送死"（人生的最后一程）重视起来，不要草率。曾子也曾说："慎终追远，民德归厚矣。"（《论语·学而》）不可否认，在漫长的封建社会，包括孟子在内的儒家对于孝道的重视有着相当积极的意义，它代表着那个时代的文明和秩序，并且，孝道中合理的成分作为中华民族传统美德一直传承至今。与此同时，我们还必须看到古代孝道中不合时宜的、落后的一面，在新时代的征程中，讲究"厚养薄葬"才是我们应该倡导树立的文明新风尚。

8.14

孟子曰："君子深造[1]之以道，欲其自得之也。自得之，则居之安；居之安，则资[2]之深；资之深，则取之左右逢其原[3]，故君子欲其自得之也。"

Mencius said, "The superior man makes his advances in what he is learning with deep earnestness and by the proper course, wishing to get hold of it as in himself. Having got hold of it in himself, he abides in it calmly and firmly. Abiding in it calmly and firmly, he reposes a deep reliance on it. Reposing a deep reliance on it, he seizes it on the left and right, meeting everywhere with it as a fountain from which things flow. It is on this account that the superior man wishes to get hold of what he is learning as in himself."

【注解】［1］深造：朱熹《四书章句集注》："深造之者，进而不已之意。"《辞源》："深造：谓达到精深的境界。也指进一步学习和研究。"［2］资：积蓄。［3］原：同"源"。

【译文】孟子说："君子依循正确的方法来深入学习和研究，是想使自己有所心得。自己有所心得，就能掌握牢固；掌握牢固，就能积蓄深厚；积蓄深厚，就能取之不尽左右逢源，所以君子希望能有所得。"

【解读】孟子在本章论述了君子做学问时要达到的三种境界。首先是"深造之以道"，即运用正确的方法，循序渐进，逐渐深入到知识的精髓中去，看清本质，掌握规律，切忌浅尝辄止、不求甚解。其次是"自得之"，在掌握了知识的本质特征和客观规律后，君子还要发挥主观能动性，将这些收获领悟于心，也就是将外在的学问转化为内在的学识，以达到融会贯通、举一反三的程度。最后是"左右逢其原"，通过努力，君子在学问上达到了"自得之"的境界，这样既能倒推出知识源出何处，又能明确如何运用所学知识，真正做到"取之不尽，用之不竭"。对于今天的我们来说，做学问也需要经历学懂、弄通、悟透、运用的过程，缺少或者颠倒任一环节，都不能说熟练掌握了某一门学问。

8.15

孟子曰："博学而详说之，将以反说约也。"

Mencius said, "In learning extensively and discussing minutely what is learned, the object of the superior man is that he may be able to go back and set forth in brief what is essential."

【译文】孟子说："广博地学习并且详细地解说，目的是融会贯通之后返归到简约上去。"

【解读】"博"与"约"是做学问的两种方法，其中，前者是知识积累的前提和基础，后者是学问研究的方向及目标，二者相辅相成。学习者将知识融会贯通后，再把其中的本质特征和规律性的东西简明直观地表达出来，进而达到"以有限驭无穷"的境界。

孟
子

8.16

孟子曰："以善服人者，未有能服人者也；
以善养人，然后能服天下。天下不心服而王者，
未之有也。"

Mencius said, "Never has he who would by his
excellence subdue men been able to subdue them.
Let a prince seek by his excellence to nourish men,
and he will be able to subdue the whole kingdom. It
is impossible that any one should become ruler of the
people to whom they have not yielded the subjection
of the heart."

【译文】孟子说："用善使人服输，没有能使
人服输的；用善涵养感化人，才能使天下的
人信服。天下的人不心悦诚服而能统治天下
的，这是从没有过的。"

【解读】孟子在本章向统治者论述修身对治国的重要作用。"善"应该是君王自觉追求的一种目的，而不能是为了达成某种目的而使用的手段。"以善服人"之"服"，意即"使人服"，这是一种带有强制意味的手段，怎么可能使人信服呢？"以善养人"之"养"，则有"熏陶、感化、滋养"之意，日复一日地施以善行，对民众普施仁政，便会慢慢聚成一股强大的道德力量，而这股力量则会潜移默化地熏陶、感化人们，久而久之，人们自然会心悦诚服。如此一来，君王赢得了民心，天下归顺便是顺理成章的事了。

8.17

孟子曰："言无实不祥。不祥之实，蔽贤者当之。"

Mencius said, "Words which are not true are inauspicious, and the words which are most truly obnoxious to the name of inauspicious, are those which throw into the shade men of talents and virtue."

【译文】孟子说："言之无物是不好的。这种不好的后果，应由阻碍任用贤者的人承担。"

【解读】孟子继承并完善了孔子的思想，他同样批判那些言过其实的小人行径，认为一个人言之无物，就会闭塞贤路，妨碍政事，就会对国家产生不利的影响。古人云："人微言轻。"这告诉我们一个人如果没有相应地位，

那么他的言论主张就容易被人忽视。但如果
"人重言轻"呢？占据高位的国家要员夸夸
其谈，不能解决实际问题，在其位不谋其政，
那么就会长期占据政治资源，而剥夺了贤者
的发言权。贤者无出，国家就无法进步。因此，
孟子认为，这种不祥的后果应该由阻碍任用
贤者的人承担。

8.18

徐子[1]曰：“仲尼亟[2]称于水，曰：‘水
哉，水哉！’何取于水也？”

孟子曰：“原泉混混[3]，不舍昼夜。盈
科[4]而后进，放乎四海，有本者如是，是之
取尔[5]。苟为无本，七八月之间雨集，沟浍[6]
皆盈；其涸也，可立而待也。故声闻[7]过情，
君子耻之。”

The disciple Xu said, "Zhongni often praised
water, saying, 'O water! O water!' What did he find
in water to praise?"

Mencius replied, "There is a spring of water;
how it gushes out! It rests not day nor night. It fills
up every hole, and then advances, flowing onto the
four seas. Such is water having a spring! It was this
which he found in it to praise. But suppose that the
water has no spring. In the seventh and eighth when

the rain falls abundantly, the channels in the fields are all filled, but their being dried up again may be expected in a short time. So a superior man is ashamed of a reputation beyond his merits."

【注释】〔1〕徐子：徐辟，孟子的学生。〔2〕亟（qì）：屡次。〔3〕原：通"源"。混混：水势盛大的样子。〔4〕科：坎。〔5〕是之取尔：宾语前置句，即"取是尔"，意思是"取这个罢了"。〔6〕浍（kuài）：田间大沟渠。〔7〕声闻：声望名誉。

【译文】徐子说："孔子多次赞叹水，说：'水啊，水啊！'水能给人什么可取之处呢？"

孟子说："水从源泉里滚滚涌出，日夜不停，填满坎洼不平之处又向前进，一直流至大海。有本源的人也如同此水，这就是孔子所看重的。如果没有本源，像七八月之间的暴雨骤集，大小沟渠全被灌满；但是它的

干涸，只要很短的时间。所以声望名誉超过
实情的，君子以此为耻。"

【解读】老子说过：上善若水。孔子也遇水则观，
"亟称于水"。古人常常以水比喻德行，孟
子也借徐辟之问，阐述自己对水的感悟。他
以水来喻人的道德品质，告诫徐辟要加强修
养，不能心存侥幸，沽名钓誉。否则，急于求成，
急于出名，就像七八月间的水一样，来也匆匆，
去也匆匆。只有通过不断的学习和修养，使
得才德与名声相称，才能实现自己的人生价
值。朱熹《观书有感》中有一名句："问渠
那得清如许？为有源头活水来。"千百年来
被人称颂，因为它揭示了世间最本质的问题：
万事万物要有本有源，才不致枯竭。本章中，
孟子抓住水源立论，比德于水，引申出为人
之道。这也警示我们不要汲汲于浮名，而应
在追求人生大道上踏踏实实下功夫。

8.19

孟子曰："人之所以异于禽兽者几希，庶民去之，君子存之。舜明于庶物，察于人伦，由仁义行，非行仁义也。"

Mencius said, "That whereby man differs from the lower animals is but small. The mass of people cast it away, while superior men preserve it. Shun clearly understood the multitude of things, and closely observed the relations of humanity. He walked along the path of benevolence and righteousness; he did not need to pursue benevolence and righteousness."

【译文】孟子说："人类区别于禽兽的地方只有很少一点，普通人抛弃了它，君子保存了它。舜明白了世间万物的道理，明察人伦关系，因此能按照仁义行事，而不是勉强施行仁义。"

【解读】孟子主张人性向善，认为人区别于低等动物的地方就在于此，因此也应该发自内心地去守护它。孟子所处的战国末期战乱不断，民不聊生，人与人之间为一点私利互相倾轧，社会秩序极度混乱，因此他主张从人的本性出发，呼吁人们像大舜一样，按照本身所拥有的仁义行事。法国思想家帕斯卡尔说："人是一根能思想的芦苇。"他认为人类与芦苇的区别就在于人类拥有独立思考的能力。东西方哲人对人性的认识是相通的，这也警示世人应该秉持善良的本性，遵从内心的美好情感，做仁义人，行仁义事。

8.20

孟子曰："禹恶旨酒而好善言。汤执中 [1]，立贤无方。文王视民如伤，望道而未之见。武王不泄迩 [2]，不忘远。周公思兼三王 [3]，以施四事 [4]；其有不合者，仰而思之，夜以继日；幸而得之，坐以待旦。"

Mencius said, "Yu hated the pleasant wine, and loved good words. Tang held fast the Mean, and employed men of talents and virtue without regard to where they came from. King Wen looked on the people as he would on a man who was wounded, and he looked towards the right path as if he could not see it. King Wu did not slight the near, and did not forget the distant. The duke of Zhou desired to unite in himself the virtues of those kings, those founders of the three dynasties, that he might display in his practice the four things which they did. If he saw

any thing in them not suited to his time, he looked
up and thought about it, from daytime into the night,
and when he was fortunate enough to master the
difficulty, he sat waiting for the morning."

【注释】［1］执中：执中正之道。［2］泄：狎侮，
轻慢。迩：近。［3］三王：夏、商、周三代
的王。［4］四事：指禹、汤、文王、武王四
人的事业。

【译文】孟子说："禹厌恶美酒而喜欢有道理
的话。汤坚持中正之道，选拔人才不按照既
定的规矩。文王将百姓当作自己需要抚慰的
伤痛来对待，渴望王道却从未见到。武王不
轻慢朝廷中的近臣，不遗忘远处的诸侯。周
公想要兼学夏、商、周三代的王，来实践禹、汤、
文王、武王所行的勋业，其中有不符合的地
方，便抬着头思考，不分昼夜；有幸得到答案，
就坐着等待天亮去付诸实践。"

【解读】本章孟子称赞禹、汤、文王、武王的德政，总结了他们各自治国理政的独特个性和原则。禹之所以"恶旨酒而好善言"，是因为酒能使人误事，是害人之物；善言虽然有时逆耳，却是治世良方。汤"执中"也就是不走极端，选才上没有偏见，也不墨守成规。文王"视民如伤"，也就是对民呵护有加，不以百姓为刍狗，一直追求着道义。武王"不泄迩，不忘远"，这是平易待人，不分亲疏远近。孟子把周公看作是兼"三代圣王"之美德的伟人。周公制礼作乐，经天纬地，是集诸圣之大成的有大功大德之人，他之所以有如此继往开来的功绩，在于既撷取前代执政中的合理部分付诸实施，又对现行制度中不合时宜的部分予以变革和创新。周公的这种开拓进取精神、不因循守旧的做法，值得我们学习。

8.21

孟子曰："王者之迹熄[1]而《诗》亡，《诗》亡然后《春秋》作。晋之《乘》，楚之《梼杌》，鲁之《春秋》[2]，一也。其事则齐桓、晋文，其文则史。孔子曰：'其义则丘窃取之矣。'"

Mencius said, "The traces of sovereign rule were extinguished, and the royal odes ceased to be made. When those odes ceased to be made, then the *Spring and Autumn* was produced. The *Sheng* of Jin, the Taowu of Chu, and the *Spring and Autumn* of Lu were books of the same character. The subject of the *Spring and Autumn* was the affairs of Huan of Qi and Wen of Jin, and its style was the historical. Confucius said. 'Its righteous decisions I ventured to make.' "

【注释】［1］王者之迹熄：指与圣王相关的一

系列礼乐文化的崩塌。[2]《乘》《梼杌》（táo wù）《春秋》：分别是晋、楚、鲁史官所记的史书书名。

【译文】孟子说："圣王的礼乐制度与秩序崩塌后《诗》也消亡了，《诗》消亡了然后《春秋》一书就出现了。晋国的《乘》，楚国的《梼杌》，鲁国的《春秋》，都是一样的。所记录的是齐桓公、晋文公（昏上乱下）一类的事，题材属于史书。孔子说：'《史书》里蕴含的褒贬的大义我汲取总结到《春秋》中了。'"

【解读】关于"王者之迹熄而《诗》亡"，史上多有争论。孟子之所以如是说，其动机是彰显或者推崇孔子作《春秋》的重大意义。《孟子·滕文公下》中说："孔子成《春秋》而乱臣贼子惧。"孔子认同《春秋》具有褒善贬恶、垂戒万世的作用，他通过对史料的甄别删减，将自己对史实的褒贬态度寓于其

中，给不同的人以不同的评价。孔子对《春秋》
的修纂体现了其伦理思想和道德判断，也使
《春秋》成为对后世进行道德教化的重要教材，
起到了对掌权者的监督和约束的效果。孟子
此章承接前两章，意在称赞孔子是那个时代
史实的集大成者，是能与舜、禹、汤、文王、
武王、周公并称的先贤圣人，同时也向我们
说明了文化发展的规律，一个新的文化形式
兴起，先前的文化形式就相应地退出历史舞
台，每个时代都有其文化传承的特色，各领
风骚数百年，这也是中华文明长盛不衰的魅
力所在。

8.22

孟子曰："君子之泽五世而斩[1]，小人之泽五世而斩。予未得为孔子徒也，予私淑[2]诸人也。"

Mencius said, "The influence of a sovereign sage terminates in the fifth generation. The influence of a mere sage does the same. Although I could not be a disciple of Confucius himself, I have endeavoured to cultivate my virtue by means of others who were."

【注释】［1］泽：恩泽。斩：断绝。［2］淑：借为"叔"，获取。"私淑"意为私自敬仰并尊之为师，但未得其亲身传授。

【译文】孟子说："君子德行的影响五代以后便断绝了，小人德行的影响五代以后便断绝

了。我没有能够成为孔子的门徒，我是私下
向别人学习孔子之道的。"

【解读】本章孟子阐述了自己对家族家风变化的
看法和认识，认为无论是君子还是小人，他
们的家族传承难以为继，五代之后就会断绝，
由此衍生了一个很有名的俗语：穷不过三代，
富不过三代。这也说明社会发展自有其运转
变化的规律，人间的富贵贫贱、更替轮转多
也符合这一规律。因此，孟子提出"生于忧患，
死于安乐"的著名论断，告诫世人不能吃老
本而不思进取。此章孟子还意在说明自己立
志向孔子学习的态度，孟子与孔子相隔百年，
自己未能亲受业于孔子之门。但他就学于子
思的门人弟子，成为孔子的"私淑"弟子，
因而得闻孔子之道。自己能成为孔子思想的
传承者，将孔子思想发扬光大，就孟子而言
是无比自豪且任重而道远的。

8.23

孟子曰："可以取，可以无取，取伤廉；可以与，可以无与，与伤惠；可以死，可以无死，死伤勇。"

Mencius said, "When it appears proper to take a thing, and afterwards not proper, to take it is contrary to moderation. When it appears proper to give a thing and afterwards not proper, to give it is contrary to kindness. When it appears proper to sacrifice one's life, and afterwards not proper, to sacrifice it is contrary to bravery."

【译文】孟子说："可以取，也可以不取，取了就有损于廉洁；可以给，也可以不给，给了就有损于恩惠；可以死，也可以不死，死了就有损于勇敢。"

【解读】与著名的"鱼与熊掌"二者必选其一不同，孟子在此章摆出的是一种两可之间的选择。对今人来说，确实是值得认真思考对待的问题。"取伤廉"比较好理解，诸如回扣吃还是不吃，红包收还是不收，收取当然会使廉洁之心受污。"与伤惠"可以这样理解，在可以给也可以不给的情况下，还是不给的好。因为孔子说"君子周急不继富"（《论语·雍也》），给了反而有滥施恩惠的嫌疑，会对实际真正需要恩惠的人有所损害。至于说"死伤勇"，是指我们在面对生死抉择的时候，其实有时活下来比死去需要更大的勇气和更强的战胜困难和耻辱的毅力。死不得其义、不得其所，这样的死，其实是缺乏勇气的表现，这就是"死伤勇"。例如司马迁为了完成《史记》，"隐忍苟活，幽于粪土之中而不辞"（《报任安书》），这其实不是怯懦，而是大勇。面对难以抉择的境况，孟子告知我们要慎思笃行，要正确理解儒家价值观。

8.24

逢蒙学射于羿^[1]，尽羿之道，思天下惟羿为愈己，于是杀羿。孟子曰："是亦羿有罪焉。"

公明仪曰："宜若^[2]无罪焉。"

曰："薄^[3]乎云尔，恶得无罪？郑人使子濯孺子^[4]侵卫，卫使庾公之斯^[5]追之。子濯孺子曰：'今日我疾作^[6]，不可以执弓，吾死矣夫！'问其仆曰：'追我者谁也？'其仆曰：'庾公之斯也。'曰：'吾生矣。'其仆曰：'庾公之斯，卫之善射者也，夫子曰'吾生'，何谓也？'曰：'庾公之斯学射于尹公之他，尹公之他学射于我。夫尹公之他，端人^[7]也，其取友必端矣。'庾公之斯至，曰：'夫子何为不执弓？'曰：'今日我疾作，不可以执弓。'曰：'小人学射于尹公之他，尹公之他学射于夫子。我不忍以夫子之道反害夫子。虽然，今日之事，君事也，我不敢废。'

抽矢扣轮，去其金 [8]，发乘矢 [9] 而后反。"

Pang Meng learned archery of Yi. When he had acquired completely all the science of Yi, he thought that in all the kingdom only Yi was superior to himself, and so he slew him. Mencius said, "In this case Yi also was to blame."

Gongming Yi indeed said, "It would appear as if he were not to be blamed."

Mencius said, "But he thereby only meant that his blame was slight. How can he be held without any blame? The people of Zheng sent Zizhuo Ru to make a stealthy attack on Wei, which sent Yugong Zhisi to pursue him. Zizhuo Ru said, 'Today I feel unwell, so that I cannot hold my bow. I am a dead man!' At the same time he asked his driver. 'Who is it that is pursuing me?' The driver said, 'It is Yugong Zhisi,' on which, he exclaimed, 'I shall live.' The driver said, 'Yugong Zhisi is the best archer of Wei, what do you mean by saying "I shall live?" ' Ru replied, 'Yugong Zhisi learned archery from Yingong Zhita, who again learned it from me. Now, Yingong Zhita is an upright man, and the friends of his selection must be upright also.' When Yugong Zhisi came up, he said, 'Master, why are you not holding your bow?' Ru answered him, 'Today I am feeling unwell, and cannot hold my bow.' On this Yugong Zhisi said, 'I learned archery from Yingong- Zhita, who again learned it from you. I cannot bear to injure you with your own science. The business of today, however, is the prince's business, which I dare not neglect.' He then took his arrows, knocked off their steel points against the carriage-wheel, discharged four of them, and returned."

【注释】［1］逄（páng）蒙：羿的学生。羿：又称后羿，传说是夏代有穷国的君主。［2］宜若：好像。［3］薄：这里是见识浅薄之义。

［4］子濯孺子：郑国大夫。［5］庾公之斯：
卫国大夫。［6］作：这里指发作。［7］端
人：正直之人。［8］金：这里指箭头。［9］
乘（shèng）矢：四支箭。

【译文】逢蒙跟羿学射箭，完全掌握了羿的箭术，
想到天下只有羿的箭术比自己强，于是便杀
死了羿。孟子说："这事羿自己也有罪。"

公明仪说："羿好像没有什么罪过。"

（孟子）说："你的话太浅薄了，怎么
能说没有罪呢？郑国派子濯孺子入侵卫国，
卫国派庾公之斯追击他。子濯孺子说：'今
天我的病发作了，不能够拿弓，我死定了！'
又问他的仆从说：'是谁在追我？'他的仆
从回答：'庾公之斯。'子濯孺子说：'我
可以活着了。'他的仆从说：'庾公之斯是
卫国著名的射手，先生反而说能活着了，这
话怎么说呢？'子濯孺子说：'庾公之斯是
向尹公之他学的射箭，尹公之他是向我学的

射箭。尹公之他是个正直的人，他所选择的朋友也一定正直。'庾公之斯追上了，问：'先生为什么不拿弓呢？'子濯孺子说：'今天我疾病发作，不能够拿弓。'庾公之斯说：'我跟尹公之他学射箭，尹公之他又跟您学射箭。我不忍心用您的箭术反过来害您。即使这样，今天这事是君王交代之事，我不敢不听。'于是抽出箭，在车轮上敲打了几下，把箭头敲掉，发了四箭然后就回去了。"

【解读】逢蒙艺成害师，令人不齿，对于这种恩将仇报的卑劣行径，人神共愤，这历来也是大家的共识。但孟子对此提出了自己的独特见解，他认为羿有自取其祸的责任，择人不淑，施教无德，结果招致杀身之祸。如果羿不只是教逢蒙箭术，还教他做人的道理，还会发生这等欺师灭祖的惨剧吗？孟子本章举了一个反例来说明对学生人品培养的重要性。作为师父，应该向子濯孺子学习，传艺更要传德，培养出德艺双馨的人，甚至在关键时刻能逢凶化吉。这对我们的启示是：选拔干部、教授学徒都要慎重选择，从德与才两个方面去教育培养，使其德才兼备、全面发展。只有一批又一批德才兼备的人不断成长，我们的民族和国家才能取得长足进步，保持繁荣富强。

8.25

孟子曰："西子[1]蒙不洁，则人皆掩鼻而过之。虽有恶[2]人，齐[3]戒沐浴，则可以祀上帝。"

Mencius said, "If the lady Xi had been covered with a filthy head-dress, all people would have stopped their noses in passing her. Though a man may be wicked, yet if he adjust his thoughts, fast, and bathe, he may sacrifice to God."

【注释】［1］西子：春秋时越国美女西施。［2］恶：指丑陋。［3］齐：通"斋"。

【译文】孟子说："像西施那样的美女要是沾染上不干净的东西，那么别人都会捂着鼻子过去。即使是面貌丑陋的人，能够斋戒沐浴，那么也可以祭祀上天。"

【解读】本章孟子用形象的对比，阐述了美丑善恶相互转化的辩证法。人的容貌来自父母，美丑与否与生俱来，不可强求。就算貌比西施，如果沾染污秽，或者懈怠放纵、行为不检，人们仍会避而远之。这启示我们先天条件再好，也不能沾沾自喜、不思进取。当然先天条件差的人，也不能自暴自弃、自甘堕落，长相丑陋的人也可以拥有虔诚美好的心灵。决定一个人的一生是否有价值在于其后天是否努力，所谓勤能补拙，不努力的人其先天的优势也会被埋没。人们通过后天道德修养的提升，具备了好的品质后，也应努力保持而不丧失。如果曾经误入歧途，就应努力改过自新，改正过错的人仍然会得到人们的认可，自我把握尤为重要。在道德修养上，学无止境、至真至善应该成为我们永恒的追求。

8.26

　　孟子曰："天下之言性也，则故^[1]而已矣。故者以利^[2]为本。所恶于智者^[3]，为其凿也。如智者若禹之行水也，则无恶于智矣。禹之行水也，行其所无事也。如智者亦行其所无事，则智亦大矣。天之高也，星辰之远也，苟求其故，千岁之日至^[4]，可坐而致也。"

Mencius said, "All who speak about the natures of things, have in fact only their phenomena to reason from, and the value of a phenomenon is in its being natural. What I dislike in your wise men is their boring out their conclusions. If those wise men would only act as Yu did when he conveyed away the waters, there would be nothing to dislike in their wisdom. The manner in which Yu conveyed away the waters was by doing what gave him no trouble. If your wise men would also do that which

gave them no trouble, their knowledge would also
be great. There is heaven so high; there are the stars
so distant. If we have investigated their phenomena,
we may, while sitting in our places, go back to the
solstice of a thousand years ago."

【注释】［1］故：本来，朱熹《孟子集注》释为"已
然之迹"。［2］利：顺应。［3］智者：巧智、
机心之意。［4］日至：冬至和夏至。

【译文】孟子说："（现今）天下人们所说的性，
就是指已有的迹象罢了。已有的迹象要以顺
应自然为根本。巧智之所以让人厌恶，是因
为它容易让人穿凿附会（不从事物本身出发）。
如果有巧智的人像大禹治水那样，那么巧智
就不被人厌恶。大禹治水，顺应水的本性，
看起来像无所作为。如果聪明人也能这样无
所作为，那就是大智慧了。天很高，星辰很远，
如果能探求它们已有运行规律的迹象，千年

以后的日至，都可以坐着推算出来了。"

【解读】本章开篇"天下之言性也，则故而已矣。故者以利为本"，是孟子针对当时社会风气而言，或者说是当时人们普遍对人性的理解，并不为孟子所赞同、认可。"以利为本"就必然让人投机取巧，耍尽小聪明，即所谓"为其凿也"。认识事物的正确方法，在于以客观实际为基础，不主观臆断、穿凿附会。顺应自然就能找到其客观规律，认清其本质。所以孟子认为认识人的本性，应根据人性的本来面目，找出其内在规律。就像大禹依照水向下流的特性而治理水患一样，因势利导，才能事成功垂。在实际生活中，总是有不少自以为很聪明的人，逆势而为，妄图逆天改命，常想一夜暴富、一日成圣，自然被生活教训得头破血流。"天之高也，星辰之远也，苟求其故，千岁之日至，可坐而致也。"孟子在这里是表达这样的一个意思：自然界的问

题与人性的问题是不同的，因而探究的方法
也不一样。万事万物都有其固有的运行规律，
我们要发挥主观能动性，找到这种规律，并
科学贯彻执行，才能不走弯路，最终收获成功。

8.27

公行子[1]有子之丧，右师[2]往吊，入门，有进而与右师言者，有就右师之位而与右师言者。孟子不与右师言，右师不悦曰："诸君子皆与驩言，孟子独不与驩言，是简[3]驩也。"

孟子闻之，曰："礼，朝廷不历位[4]而相与言，不逾阶而相揖也。我欲行礼，子敖以我为简，不亦异乎？"

The officer Gonghang having on hand the funeral of one of his sons, the Master of the Right went to condole with him. When this noble entered the door, some called him to them and spoke with him, and some went to his place and spoke with him. Mencius did not speak with him, so that he was displeased, and said, "All the gentlemen have spoken with me. There is only Mencius who does not speak to me, thereby slighting me."

Mencius, having heard of this remark, said, "According to the prescribed rules, in the court, individuals may not change their places to speak with one another, nor may they pass from their ranks to bow to one another. I was wishing to observe this rule, and Ziao understands it that I was slighting him: —is not this strange?"

【注释】［1］公行子：人名，齐国大夫。［2］右师：先秦时期官名，此处指齐国大夫王驩，字子敖。［3］简：这里是怠慢的意思。［4］历位：越位。

【译文】公行子的儿子死了，右师前往吊丧，进了门，有上前和右师交谈的人，有靠近右师座位与右师交谈的人。孟子不和右师说话，右师不高兴地说："诸位大人都和我交谈，唯独孟子不和我交谈，是怠慢我。"

孟子听到这话，说："依礼，在朝廷上

不能越过位置相互交谈，不能越过台阶相互作揖行礼。我依礼而行，子敖却认为我怠慢他，不也是很奇怪吗？"

【解读】本章这个事例，表现了孟子以礼待人、不趋炎附势的高尚节操和品格。右师王驩作为齐国大夫，认为自己位高权重，孟子在吊丧时没有与之交谈，就心怀不满，认为这是怠慢他。而孟子认为自己遵循礼制，在朝廷上不应越过位置交谈。二者相较，修养之高下自明。做人不能自高自大、凌驾一切，一旦狂妄忘形，往往会自取其辱。

孟子是忠诚守礼的卫道者，知礼守礼的思想在其内心根深蒂固。他的行为在当时确实值得称赞，但于今日而言，不免有些迂腐死板、不知变通。当我们在一些重要的场合或活动中遇到领导、同事时，主动打招呼还是必要的，只不过要注意场合和自己的仪态，把握好尺度即可。

8.28

孟子曰："君子所以异于人者，以其存心[1]也。君子以仁存心，以礼存心。仁者爱人，有礼者敬人。爱人者人恒爱之，敬人者人恒敬之。有人于此，其待我以横逆[2]，则君子必自反[3]也：我必不仁也，必无礼也，此物奚宜[4]至哉？其自反而仁矣，自反而有礼矣，其横逆由[5]是也，君子必自反也：我必不忠。自反而忠矣，其横逆由是也，君子曰：'此亦妄人也已矣。如此则与禽兽奚择[6]哉？于禽兽又何难[7]焉？'是故君子有终身之忧，无一朝之患也。乃若[8]所忧则有之：舜人也，我亦人也。舜为法[9]于天下，可传于后世，我由未免为乡人[10]也，是则可忧也。忧之如何？如舜而已矣。若夫君子所患则亡矣。非仁无为也，非礼无行也。如有一朝之患，则君子不患矣。"

Mencius said, "That whereby the superior man is distinguished from other men is what he preserves in his heart; —namely, benevolence and propriety. The benevolent man loves others. The man of propriety shows respect to others. He who loves others is constantly loved by them. He who respects others is constantly respected by them. Here is a man, who treats me in a perverse and unreasonable manner. The superior man in such a case will turn round upon himself— 'I must have been wanting in benevolence; I must have been wanting in propriety—how should this have happened to me?' He examines himself, and is specially benevolent. He turns round upon himself, and is specially observant of propriety. The perversity and unreasonableness of the other, however, are still the same. The superior man will again turn round on himself, 'I must have been failing to do my utmost.' He turns round upon himself,and proceeds to do his utmost, but still the perversity and unreasonableness of the other are repeated. On this the superior man says, 'This is a man utterly lost indeed! Since he conducts himself so, what is there to choose between him and a brute? Why should I go to contend with a brute?' Thus it is that the superior man has a life-long anxiety and not one morning's calamity. As to what is matter of anxiety to him, that indeed he has. He says, 'Shun was a man, and I also am a man. But Shun became all example to all the kingdom, and his conduct was worthy to be handed down to after ages, while I am nothing better than a villager.' This indeed is the proper matter of anxiety to him. And in what way is he anxious about it? Just that he maybe like Shun: then only will he stop. As to what the superior man would feel to be a calamity, there is no such thing. He does nothing which is not according to propriety. If there should befall him one morning's calamity, the superior man does not account it a calamity."

【注释】［1］存心：仁爱、礼义存于心。［2］横逆：蛮横无理。［3］自反：自我反思。［4］奚宜：怎么应当。［5］由：通"犹"，仍然，还是。［6］择：区别。［7］何难：有什么可责难。难：责难。［8］乃若：至于，比如。［9］法：楷模。［10］乡人：普通人。

【译文】孟子说："君子之所以与一般人不同，在于他内心所怀的念头。君子把仁放在心上，把礼放在心上。仁人爱别人，有礼的人尊敬别人。爱别人的人，别人也常爱他；尊敬别人的人，别人也常尊敬他。有个人在这里，他对我蛮横无理，那君子必定反思自问：我一定不仁，一定无理吧，否则这件事怎么落到我的身上呢？如果反躬自问后认为自己是仁的，是有礼的，那人仍然蛮横无理，君子必定反躬自问：我一定不忠吧。如果反躬自问后认为自己是忠的，而那人仍然蛮横无理，君子就会说：'这人不过是个狂人罢了。像这样的人，和禽兽有什么区别呢？又有什么可责难禽兽的呢？'所以君子有终身的忧虑，但没有一朝一夕的祸患。至于这样终身忧虑的事是有的：舜是人，我也是人。舜是天下人的楷模，名声传于后世，我却不免是一个普通人，这个是值得忧虑的事。忧虑又怎么办呢？像舜那样做罢了。至于君子忧患的事，就没有了。不是仁爱的事不为，不合于礼的事不做。即使有一朝一夕的祸患，君子也不会感到忧患了。"

【解读】本章是典型的劝人互敬互爱的文字，孟子在论述中强调了个人修养中的反躬自省，告诉我们即使自己受到不公正的对待时，也要反省自己的不足，而不应以牙还牙。俗语"静坐常思己过，闲谈莫论人非"，也是警示我们要反思自己待人处事时疏忽和欠缺的地方，避免以后犯同样的错误，这样就会减少对他人的怨恨。道理好懂，关键是在实践中应有如此积极的行动。如果人人都能做到像文中的君子一样，许多人世间的矛盾瓜葛自然会迎刃而解。需要补充的是，孟子主张遇到蛮横无理的对待时首先要反省自己，并不是对道德原则的否定，如果自己并无过错，那就要坚持原则，威武不屈。对于那些丧尽天良、蛮横无理的狂妄之徒，我们当然不能妥协退让，而应据理力争，维护社会的公平正义。

8.29

禹、稷当平世[1]，三过其门而不入，孔子贤之。颜子[2]当乱世，居于陋巷。一箪食，一瓢饮，人不堪其忧，颜子不改其乐，孔子贤之。孟子曰："禹、稷、颜回同道。禹思天下有溺者，由己溺之也；稷思天下有饥者，由己饥之也，是以如是其急也。禹、稷、颜子易地则皆然。今有同室之人斗者，救之，虽被[3]发缨冠而救之，可也。乡邻有斗者，被发缨冠而往救之，则惑也，虽闭户可也。"

Yu and Ji, in an age when the world was being brought back to order, thrice passed their doors without entering them. Confucius praised them. The disciple Yan, in an age of disorder, dwelt in a mean narrow lane, having his single bamboo-cup of rice, and his single gourd-dish of water; other men could not have endured the distress, but he did not allow his joy to be affected by it. Confucius praised him. Mencius said, "Yu, Ji, and Yan Hui agreed in the principle of their conduct. Yu thought that if any one in the kingdom were drowned, it was as if he drowned him. Ji thought that if any one in the kingdom suffered hunger, it was as if he famished him. It was on this account that they were so earnest. If Yu and Ji, and Yanzi, had exchanged places, each would have done what the other did. Here now in the same apartment with you are people fighting: — you ought to part them. Though you part them with your cap simply tied over your unbound hair, your conduct will be allowable. If the fighting be only in the village or neighbourhood, if you go to put an end to it with your cap tied over your hair unbound, you will be in error. Although you should shut your door in such a case, your conduct would be allowable."

【注释】［1］平世：太平盛世。［2］颜子：孔子弟子颜回。［3］被：同"披"。

【译文】 禹、稷生活在太平盛世中，多次经过自己家门却没进去，孔子称赞他们。颜回处于乱世中，住在简陋的巷子里，一筐饭，一瓢水，别人忍受不了那样的穷苦，颜回却自得其乐，孔子也称赞他。孟子说："禹、稷、颜回都是同样的道理。禹思虑着天下有遭到水淹的人，就像是自己使他们淹没了一样；稷思虑着天下有挨饿的人，就像是自己使他们挨饿了一样，因此他们急切地拯救百姓。禹、稷、颜回若交换处境也会有同样的做法。现在假设有同屋的人斗殴，要去救他们，即使披散头发连帽缨也不系就去救，也是可以的；若乡邻之间有斗殴的，也披散头发连帽缨也不系就去救，那就是糊涂了，即使关门闭户也是可以的。"

【解读】 本章孟子以禹、稷、颜回三人的例子

禹、稷三过其门而不入　李岩　绘

论述个人在道德修养上的坚守，即使是环境不同，时空地位互换，孟子判断他们也会做出同样的选择。禹、稷身处盛世依然胸怀天下，推己及人般地心系民众疾苦；颜回身处乱世就修身养性、安贫乐道，二者都是出于"仁"的本义，因此同样得到了孔子的称赞，这与孔子的"忠恕"之道是相通的。孟子认为，做人做事，要依"道"而行，"进则救民，退则修己"（朱熹《四书章句集注》）。虽然每个人所处的地位、环境不同，内心对仁义的追求却应该是相同的，这与其在《孟子·尽心上》中提到的"穷则独善其身，达则兼善天下"是一个道理。这也启示我们不论身处何种境地，都要严格要求自己，积极培养自身的道德修养，坚定意志，胸怀理想，无愧人生。

8.30

公都子曰："匡章[1]，通国皆称不孝焉。夫子与之游，又从而礼貌之，敢问何也？"

孟子曰："世俗所谓不孝者五：惰其四支[2]，不顾父母之养，一不孝也；博弈好饮酒，不顾父母之养，二不孝也；好货财，私妻子，不顾父母之养，三不孝也；从耳目之欲，以为父母戮[3]，四不孝也；好勇斗很[4]，以危父母，五不孝也。章子有一于是乎？夫章子，子父责善而不相遇也。责善，朋友之道也；父子责善，贼恩之大者。夫章子，岂不欲有夫妻子母之属哉？为得罪于父，不得近。出妻屏[5]子，终身不养焉。其设心以为不若是，是则罪之大者，是则章子已矣。"

The disciple Gongdu said, "Throughout the whole kingdom everybody pronounces Kuang-zhang unfilial. But you, Master, keep company with him, and moreover treat him with politeness. I venture to ask why you do so."

Mencius replied, "There are five things which are pronounced in the common usage of the age to be unfilial. The first is laziness in the use of one's four limbs, without attending to the nourishment of his parents. The second is gambling and chess-playing, and being fond of wine, without attending to the nourishment of his parents. The third is being fond of goods and money, and selfishly attached to his wife and children, without attending to the nourishment of his parents. The fourth is following the desires of one's ears and eyes, so as to bring his parents to disgrace. The fifth is being fond of bravery, fighting and quarrelling so as to endanger his parents. Is Zhang guilty of any one of these things? Now between Zhang and his father there arose disagreement, he, the son, reproving his father, to urge him to what was good. To urge one another to what is good by reproofs is the way of friends. But such urging between father and son is the greatest injury to the kindness, which should prevail between them. Moreover, did not Zhang wish to have in his family the relationships of husband and wife, child and mother? But because he had offended his father, and was not permitted to approach him, he sent away his wife, and drove forth his son, and all his life receives no cherishing attention from them. He settled it in his mind that if he did not act in this way, his would be one of the greatest of crimes. Such and nothing more is the case of Zhang."

【注释】［1］匡章：齐国著名战将，孟子的学生。［2］支：同"肢"。［3］戮：羞辱。［4］很：通"狠"，凶狠。［5］屏：摒弃，疏远。

【译文】公都子说："匡章这个人，全国都说他不孝。您与他交往，又礼貌地对待他，请问这是为什么呢？"

孟子说："世俗所说的不孝有五种：四肢懒惰，不照顾父母的生活，这是不孝之一；喜欢赌博喝酒，不照顾父母的生活，这是不孝之二；喜欢钱财，偏爱妻子儿女，不照顾父母的生活，这是不孝之三；放纵耳朵和眼睛的欲望，寻欢作乐，给父母蒙羞，这是不孝之四；凶勇好斗，以致危害父母，这是不孝之五。章子有犯其中的哪一种吗？章子是因为父子间劝免从善而相责才不能一起相处的。为善相责，是朋友的相处之道；父子间为善相责是大伤感情的事情。章子难道不想有夫妻母子的团聚归属吗？是因为得罪了父亲才不能亲近他，并把妻儿赶出家门，终身不得他们侍奉。他心里认为如果不受这样的惩罚，就是更大的罪过，这就是章子罢了。"

【解读】孟子对匡章礼貌相待的态度引发了公都子的困惑，故有本章一问。匡章是一位悲剧性人物,他是齐国著名将领,最后做出了"出妻屏子"的举动来惩罚自己。由此引发了孟子的"不孝有五"之说。前章提及"不孝有三,无后为大",故而学术界对此有较多的分歧,但多认同"不孝有五"的论断。无论不孝有三还是有五,孟子特别重视孝道是无疑的。全国人都说匡章不孝,孟子却认为这是他因为父子之间因善相责而导致如此后果,并不属于五种不孝的情形之一。对于人云亦云的事情应该有自己独立的思考和判断,对于一个人的评价,不能简单地根据道听途说就盲目下结论。这个故事提醒我们,人应该根据客观实际情况有自己清醒的分析判断,对于任何事情都不能偏听偏信,应该进行仔细观察与考证、分析与研究,不被表面所迷惑,不被他人所误导。本章所提及的五种不孝,对当今社会的人们依然具有很大的警示作用,其冲击力之强,可能会让许多人汗颜,故而有着积极的现实意义。

8.31

　　曾子居武城^[1]，有越寇。或曰："寇至，盍去诸？"曰："无寓人于我室，毁伤其薪木。"寇退，则曰："修我墙屋，我将反。"寇退，曾子反。左右曰："待先生，如此其忠且敬也。寇至则先去以为民望，寇退则反，殆于不可。"

　　沈犹行^[2]曰："是非汝所知也。昔沈犹有负刍之祸^[3]，从先生者七十人，未有与焉。"

　　子思居于卫，有齐寇。或曰："寇至，盍去诸？"子思曰："如伋去，君谁与守？"

　　孟子曰："曾子、子思同道。曾子，师也，父兄也；子思，臣也，微也。曾子、子思易地则皆然。"

When the philosopher Zeng dwelt in Wu-cheng, there came a band from Yue to plunder it. Someone said to him, "The plunderers are coming: —why not leave this?" Zeng on this left the city, saying to the man in charge of the house, "Do not lodge any persons in my house, lest they break and injure the plants and trees." When the plunderers withdrew, he sent word to him, saying, "Repair the walls of my house. I am about to return." When the plunderers retired, the philosopher Zeng returned accordingly. His disciples said, "Since our master was treated with so much sincerity and respect, for him to be the first to go away on the arrival of the plunderers, so as to be observed by the people, and then to return on their retiring, appears to us to be improper."

Shenyou Xing said, "You do not understand this matter. Formerly, when Shenyou was exposed to the outbreak of the grass-carriers, there were seventy disciples in our master's following, and none of them took part in the matter."

When Zisi was living in Wei, there came a band from Qi to plunder. Some one said to him, "The

孟
子

plunderers are coming; —why not leave this?' Zi-si said, "If I go away, whom will the prince have to guard the state with?"

Mencius said, "The philosophers Zeng and Zi-si agreed in the principle of their conduct. Zeng was a teacher; —in the place of a father or elder brother. Zisi was a minister; —in a meaner place. If the philosophers Zeng and Zisi had exchanged places, the one would have done what the other did."

【注释】[1]武城:地名,在今山东费县西南。[2]沈犹行:人名,曾子的学生。[3]负刍（chú）:指砍柴打草,一说为人名。负刍之祸指砍柴打草的穷人们起来造反,或指一位叫负刍的人发动的叛乱。

【译文】曾子住在武城,有越国的流寇侵犯。有人说:"流寇来了,何不离开呢?"

（曾子）说:"不要让人住我的房子,

不要毁坏了这里的树木。"流寇退走了，曾子就说："修理我的墙屋，我将回去。"流寇退走了，曾子就返回。身边的学生们说："人们对待您是如此的忠诚和恭敬啊，流寇来了，您却先行离开做了这样一个榜样；流寇退走，就返回来，大概不太合适吧？"

沈犹行说："这不是你们所了解的。从前我曾遭遇过负刍之祸，跟随老师的七十个人全都躲避开了。"

子思居住在卫国，有齐国的流寇来进犯。有人说："流寇来了，何不离开呢？"子思说："如果我孔伋走了，卫君和谁来守城呢？"

孟子说："曾子、子思的主张是一致的。曾子，是老师，是父兄一样的长辈；子思，是臣下，是小官。曾子、子思如果互换位置也会这样做。"

【解读】本章故事中，曾子遇寇而退，子思遇寇而守，到底谁对谁错呢？孟子认为，曾子是老师长辈，遇有寇来，弟子怎能让老师冲锋陷阵呢？因此曾子选择离开，是为了使弟子一心抗敌。而子思当时是卫国官员，臣子有守土之责，当然不能擅离职守。二者互换地位，也会做出一样的选择。这就告诉我们遇事应灵活应对，不能照本宣科，不同情境下遇到类似的情况可以有不同的处理方式。

"变"是事物发展的规律，"应变"是一个人能力的表现，当然还要看你的职责所在，灵活变通并不是牺牲职业道德，而是审时度势，选择适当的行为方式去应对。

8.32

储子[1]曰："王使人瞯[2]夫子，果有以异于人乎？"

孟子曰："何以异于人哉？尧、舜与人同耳。"

The officer Chu said to Mencius, "Master, the king sent persons to spy out whether you were really different from other men."

Mencius said, "How should I be different from other men? Yao and Shun were just the same as other men."

【注释】［1］储子：齐国人。齐宣王时曾为相。［2］瞯（jiàn）：窥伺，偷看。

【译文】储子说："君王派人来观察您，您果然有不同于常人的地方吗？"

孟子说："我哪里有什么不同于常人的呢？尧、舜也同普通人一样罢了。"

【解读】《论语·子罕》中，也有类似本章这样的疑问——"太宰问于子贡曰：'夫子圣者与？何其多能也？'"大概齐国的君王也想窥伺一下孟子有何异于常人之处，于是储子像太宰感慨孔子的多能一样，发出疑问。孟子的回答是，人皆可为尧舜，这无疑发出了"人人皆平等"的先声。普通人在道德修养上，可以与圣人一样通过努力内修达到至圣至善的境界。这种基于人格平等的理论，对于鼓励人们发挥个人主观能动性、实现理想人格创造了可能，这也是孟子内圣功夫深受后人推崇的原因。

8.33

齐人有一妻一妾而处室者，其良人 [1] 出，则必餍 [2] 酒肉而后反。其妻问所与饮食者，则尽富贵也。其妻告其妾曰：“良人出，则必餍酒肉而后反；问其与饮食者，尽富贵也，而未尝有显者来，吾将瞷良人之所之也。”

蚤 [3] 起，施 [4] 从良人之所之，遍国中 [5] 无与立谈者。卒之东郭墦[6]间，之祭者，乞其余；不足，又顾而之他，此其为餍足之道也。

其妻归，告其妾曰：“良人者，所仰望而终身也。今若此。”与其妾讪 [7] 其良人，而相泣于中庭。而良人未之知也，施施 [8] 从外来，骄其妻妾。

由君子观之，则人之所以求富贵利达者，其妻妾不羞也，而不相泣者，几希矣。

A man of Qi had a wife and a concubine, and lived together with them in his house. When their husband went out, he would get himself well filled with wine and flesh, and then return, and, on his wife's asking him with whom he ate and drank, they were sure to be all wealthy and honourable people. The wife informed the concubine, saying, "When our good man goes out, he is sure to come back having partaken plentifully of wine and flesh. I asked with whom he ate and drank, and they are all, it seems, wealthy and honourable people. And yet no people of distinction ever come here. I will spy out where our good man goes."

Accordingly, she got up early in the morning, and privately followed wherever her husband went. Throughout the whole city, there was no one who stood or talked with him. At last, he came to those who were sacrificing among the tombs beyond the outer wall on the east, and begged what they had over. Not being satisfied, he looked about, and went to another party; —and this was the way in which he got himself satiated.

His wife returned, and informed the concubine, saying, "It was to our husband that we looked up in hopeful contemplation, with whom our lot is cast for life; — and now these are his ways!" On this, along with the concubine she reviled their husband, and they wept together in the middle hall. In the meantime the husband, knowing nothing of all this, came in with a jaunty air, carrying himself proudly to his wife and concubine.

In the view of a superior man, as to the ways by which men seek for riches, honours, gain, and advancement, there are few of their wives and concubines who would not be ashamed and weep together on account of them.

【注释】［1］良人：古代妇女对丈夫的称呼。［2］餍（yàn）：饱。［3］蚤：同"早"。［4］施：这里指暗中跟随，以免被丈夫发现。［5］国中：都城中。［6］墦（fán）：坟墓。［7］讪：
讥诮，讥骂。［8］施施：得意洋洋的样子。

【译文】齐国有个人，家有一妻一妾，丈夫每
次出门，吃饱肉、喝足酒才回家。他妻子问
他一块吃喝的是什么人，（他说）全都是些
有钱有势的人。他妻子告诉他的妾说："丈
夫每次出门，都是吃饱肉、喝足酒才回来；
问他和什么人一块吃喝，全都是有钱有势的
人，但从来没有显贵的人到家里来过，我打
算偷偷地看看他到底去了什么地方。"

一早起来，她便尾随在丈夫的后面，走
遍全城，不见一人停下来和他说话。最后他
走到了东郊的墓地，向祭扫坟墓的人要些剩
余的祭品吃；不够又东张西望地到别处去乞
讨，这就是他吃饱肉、喝足酒的办法。

妻子回到家里，告诉妾说："丈夫，是
我们仰望而托付终身的人，现在竟然这样！"
于是便与妾讥骂她们的丈夫，进而在院子里

哭了起来。然而她们的丈夫还不知道，得意洋洋地从外面回来，在两个女人面前摆威风。

在君子看来，人们用来求取富贵利达的方法，能够不使他们的妻妾引以为耻而互相哭泣的，是很少的。

【解读】本章采用讽刺小品的形式，描述向祭奠者乞食的齐人之卑劣形象，其目的在于讽刺那些为求富贵权势不择手段、不顾廉耻的人。孔子说："不义而富且贵，于我如浮云。"(《论语·述而》)追求名利地位、财富权势无可厚非，但这种追求应该建立在符合道义的基础之上。如果像故事中的齐人一样虚伪，自欺欺人，丧失人格和尊严，为求酒足饭饱而摇尾乞食，着实令人不齿。爱慕虚荣的人，往往自吹自擂，装模作样，如同南郭先生滥竽充数一样，迟早会有牛皮吹破、真相败露的一天，成为大家的笑柄。当今社会，仍然有不少这类求利者、求名者，这类人的行径，如果和本章的齐人一样，就连最亲近的人都会深以为耻。本章所述的故事，警示世人须看破虚妄名利，沽名钓誉往往会导致人生的悲剧。

后记

　　"中华优秀传统文化书系"是山东省委宣传部组织实施的 2019 年山东省优秀传统文化传承发展工程重点项目，由山东出版集团、山东画报出版社策划出版。

　　"中华优秀传统文化书系"由曲阜彭门创作室彭庆涛教授担任主编，高尚举、孙永选、刘岩、郭云鹏、李岩担任副主编。特邀孟祥才、杨朝明、臧知非、孟继新等教授担任学术顾问。书系采用朱熹《四书章句集注》与《十三经注疏》为底本，英文对照主要参考理雅各（James Legge）经典翻译版本。

　　《孟子》（二）由刘岩担任执行主编；

朱宁燕、黄秀韬、王新莹、尚树志担任主撰；
王明朋、朱振秋、刘建、李金鹏、杨光、束
天昊、张勇、张博、陈阳光、周茹茹、房政伟、
屈士峰、高天健、郭耀、曹帅、龚昌华、韩振、
鲁慧参与本册编写工作；于志学、吴泽浩、
张仲亭、韩新维、岳海波、梁文博、韦辛夷、
徐永生、卢冰、吴磊、杨文森、杨晓刚、张博、
李岩等艺术家创作插图；本书编写过程中参
阅了大量资料，得到了众多专家学者的帮助，
在此一并致谢。